HOW TO
WRITE & SELL
GREETING CARDS,

BUMPER STICKERS,

T-SHIRTS AND OTHER FUN STUFF

ABOUT THE AUTHOR

Molly Wigand is a full-time freelance writer who provides concepts and writing to gift and greeting card companies across the country. A former writer and editor for Hallmark Cards, Wigand works as a consultant to various corporations, conducting brainstorms and giving editorial advice. She also teaches classes and seminars for aspiring greeting card creators.

HOW TO
WRITE & SELL
GREETING CARDS,

BUMPER STICKERS,

T-SHIRTS AND OTHER FUN STUFF

MOLLY WIGAND

Writer's
Digest
Books

Cincinnati, Ohio

96 95 94 93 92   5 4 3 2

Library of Congress Cataloging-in-Publication Data

Wigand, Molly
    How to write and sell greeting cards, bumper stickers, T-shirts, and other fun stuff / by Molly Wigand.
        p.   cm.
    Includes bibliographical references and index.
    ISBN 0-89879-471-4
    1. Authorship. 2. Greeting cards—Authorship. 3. Authorship—Marketing. 4. Creative ability in business. I. Title.
PN171.G74W54   1992
808'.02—dc20   91-43179
                                                CIP

Designed by Kristi Cullen

TABLE OF CONTENTS

DEDICATION

To Charlie, Joey, and Danny
with all my love.

ACKNOWLEDGMENTS

This book would not have been possible without the inspiration and instruction provided by my former colleagues at Hallmark Cards.

I also am grateful to my present associates, especially John Overmyer, Becky Rhodes, and Sue Ross, for welcoming me into their creative communities and sharing with me their extensive knowledge of the social expression industry.

I wish to extend my thanks to my editor, Nan Dibble, for sticking with me through the unusual evolution of this book; and to Bill Brohaugh for his insightful suggestions and comments.

And finally, I wish to thank my husband, Steve Jackson, whose love and support keep me going.

TABLE OF CONTENTS

Welcome to the Wonderful World of Greeting Cards, Bumper Stickers, T-Shirts and Other Fun Stuff

CHAPTER ONE

An Introduction to Social Expression Writing

uring my tenure as a writer and editor for Hallmark Cards, it became obvious to me that talented writers can come from anywhere. The company recruited writers at colleges and universities. They tried ad agencies and newspapers. And while they had *some* luck there, they also wound up hiring a cashier, a mathematician, a dental assistant, a rock musician, an ex-nun, a drywall installer, a biologist, a secretary, and an elementary school teacher. And even a psychiatric nurse (who came in very handy at times!).

All types of people, from all types of backgrounds, from all over the country. But they all possessed one very special talent: the ability to tap into the feelings — love, friendship, sorrow, joy — of the American consumer.

If you think you've got that talent, this book will give you everything else you need to write good, strong, sellable social expression products.

WHAT IS SOCIAL EXPRESSION?

The term *social expression product* refers to any product containing a "me-to-you" or "me-to-the-world" message. Greeting cards are the most ubiquitous of social expression products, but bumper stickers, buttons, mugs and message T-shirts are just a few of the other products provided by the social expression industry.

To demonstrate the current explosion in this industry, I'd like to take you on an imaginary trip to your local shopping mall. The most obvious place to find social expression products is at the card shops (sometimes known as gift shops) — Hallmark, Carleton or others. In these shops, we find cards (naturally!), but we also find "self-expression products," such as posters, calendars, mugs and buttons, to name just a few.

Now let's look more closely at this retail setting. We see a young woman wearing a faded T-shirt proclaiming "I'm With Stupid." Browsing the card racks with her are a "Sexy Senior Citizen," a "Pumping Iron" enthusiast, and a cute, little small-fry whose shirt proclaims "Look Out — Here Comes Trouble!" A teenage girl has laid a "Love Me, Love My Car" key ring on a sales counter as she writes a check from her "WARNING: DISASTER AREA" checkbook.

Strolling through a large department store, we find pajamas ("Cuddle Me!"), pot holders ("Kiss the Chef"), and even men's underwear ("Home of the Whopper") with clever messages and humorous designs.

Next we walk to the car and see a barrage of bumper stickers plastered on an old Super Beetle: "So-and-So for President," "Save the Whales," and "The Best Man for the Job Is Usually a Woman."

Driving home, we pass a delivery car filled with black "Over the Hill" helium balloons. There's a house plastered with "It's a Boy" banners. A neighbor's sign warns us, "Don't even *think* about parking here!"

Finally, we make it home through this proliferation of slogans and messages.

But wait. What's this in *my* home? *More* social expression? I don't think of myself as being a heavy user of these types of products, but an inventory of my household yields:

- Three wall calendars
- Two desk calendars
- Fifteen message buttons (large and small)
- Six posters
- A drawerful of all-purpose greeting cards
- Three pads of humorous self-stick notes
- Four plaques
- Five humorous or inspirational refrigerator magnets
- Massive quantities of message T-shirts in adult and boys' sizes

That's a lot of social expression. Many of us feel the need to express ourselves publicly, cleverly and eloquently; that's why there is such a large demand for good social expression writing. You no doubt have hundreds of good ideas and plenty of raw talent. After reading this book, you'll also have the specific tools needed for creating top-notch social expression products.

Why Do People Need Greeting Cards?

In our culture, greeting cards have become the art and poetry of the masses. For every one person out there buying an art poster in a museum store, probably ten thousand or more are buying greeting cards. For every literature lover buying a copy of Blake's poetry, probably another ten thousand consumers are buying another ten thousand cards.

People send cards when they want to do something more special or memorable than calling on the phone, but don't have the time or the inclination to write a letter.

There are two major reasons for sending greeting cards:

1. *To observe occasions or events*, such as birthdays, holidays, weddings or anniversaries. These cards tend to be "receiver intensive," that is, they focus on the life events and/or personal attributes of the *recipient* of the card.

2. *To share feelings*, such as love, friendship, pride and camaraderie, with the recipient. These cards tend to be "sender intensive," that is, they focus on the message the *sender* feels a need to express.

Whether they're funny or sad, seasonal or everyday, cutesy or intense, greeting cards make it more convenient for people to show they care. Or, as a former Hallmark boss once told me, greeting card writers "make it easier for people to be nice to each other."

This challenge—providing words to help others communicate— makes writing greeting cards a rewarding and worthwhile endeavor. Fortunately for us, it's also fun!

Why Do People Need Self-Expression Products?

In an increasingly homogenized society, we all look for ways to express our uniqueness as individuals. And for many consumers, self-expression products, such as bumper stickers, buttons and T-shirts, provide just such an opportunity to make a statement.

While greeting cards will usually have a me-to-you message, self-expression writing tends to have a me-to-the-rest-of-the-world quality. If you have a talent for coining a phrase or for zeroing in on the trends and mindsets of the moment, your slogans and mottos may meet the needs of American consumers.

Both the greeting card and the self-expression fields are excellent markets for creative writers. And whether you're writing cards for individual sale to large card companies, creating product lines on a royalty basis, or producing your own products to distribute and sell, the field of social expression writing is filled with opportunities.

During the twelve years I've worked in the industry, I've seen things change dramatically. I'm sure you, as a consumer, have seen some of these changes yourself.

Before the 1980s, a few giants—Hallmark, American Greetings, Gibson Greetings—dominated the marketplace. But during the mid- to late-'70s, something different started happening—something that revolutionized the industry and changed it permanently. A few smaller companies started offering cards and other products aimed at specific target markets. (A target market is a particular segment of consumers—e.g., working women between the ages of eighteen and thirty-five—for whom a product is specifically created.)

Also, very important, a good many of these "new" products sounded and looked totally different. Up until then, most of the merchandise in card shops had been formal and standardized: traditional verse, classically styled prose, flowery artwork. Even the humor cards were obvious gags—a setup on the outside and the punch line or payoff on the inside.

But these new products were something else. They were informal, they were feminine, they broke rules, they were risqué, they were silly, they were conversational, they were honest—and they were selling like hotcakes!

They've come to be known as "alternative" cards, posters, bumper stickers and stationery, simply because they were considered to be an alternative to the "traditional" social expression products.

How Will This Book Help Me?

In this book, you'll learn how to write both traditional and alternative copy. You'll learn how to write for greeting cards and self-expression products (the "other fun stuff" mentioned in the book's title: T-shirts, mugs, bumper stickers, buttons, posters, calendars, plaques, notepads and hats).

In addition to giving you precise directions and tips for writing all different kinds of greeting cards and other social expression products, this book includes specific hints on how to get started as a freelancer.

You'll learn how to approach editors and creative directors, how to keep track of your sales and rejections, and where to get your ideas in the first place.

The final section of the book is a mini-workbook, a compilation of exercises and idea starters to help you avoid writer's block and get past any hesitation you might feel about starting to write.

Writing for these products is fun and therapeutic, and it's almost impossible to think of it as "work." You can write a card in thirty seconds (although some seem to take thirty years!). You can write while you vacuum, shop, exercise, change a diaper, watch the soaps, wait on the telephone—I've even written them in my sleep! It's a fun and potentially lucrative hobby; and if you succeed, it's a rewarding and challenging career.

I guess you can tell . . . I like writing these cards and "other fun stuff."

The best advice I can give you is *just keep writing*. You are bound to meet obstacles and discouragements as you begin writing and selling cards, but you're bound to find satisfaction and pleasure, too. You'll feel the euphoric sensation of creating a timely, high-quality product. And with a little luck, someday, on some future trip to the mall, some of the products you see people buying (or sending or displaying) will be *your* social expression products—*your* cards, posters, T-shirts and bumper stickers.

Remember, no writer can write everything well; and the styles that come easiest to you are probably those you'll have the most success with. There's an old saying that goes, "If it ain't fun, you ain't doing it right!"

With that in mind, let's start writing!

CHAPTER TWO

It Takes All Kinds of Writing

In this chapter, I'm going to take you through the actual mental process of writing social expression copy, from generating ideas to putting them into marketable words. I'll also describe some important concepts in social expression: "empathy," "tone," "sendability," "giftability" and "allegory."

Whether you write traditional birthday cards or wacky T-shirts, the creative process is very nearly the same.

How Does the Writing Actually Happen?

Most writers do certain things, consciously and unconsciously, that are part of the creative process. I've compiled a checklist of procedures that work for most writers for most types of writing.

Remember, these are general tips that should work for any type of creative writing on almost any assignment. The tips for writing the specific styles (verse, humor, conversational prose, etc.) will be given in the chapters that specifically deal with those types of cards. But before you start to write, you have to know whom you're writing for.

Know Your Market

The market consists of the people who will buy the cards. Who is this person looking at your writing as she's card shopping? Is she young? Is she old? (Since well over 90 percent of greeting card purchasers are female, it is more appropriate to use the pronoun "she" when discussing our consumers.)

Market knowledge will come from four major sources: your editor, the media, the industry, and you.

Your Editor

In almost all of your dealings with greeting card and other social expression companies, you will establish and maintain contact with an editor. This is the person to whom you send your writing. This is also the person you hope will like it, accept it, and send you money for it. (*Hint*: Be nice to this person.)

Many of the larger companies publish *needs lists* on a regular basis, which, besides telling you exactly what kinds of cards they currently buy, often have a lot of good market information. (A sample needs list is included in the Workbook section on page 191.)

This information might include:

1. The sender's and receiver's age range, sex (probably female), marital status, income level, social status, etc. This information is often referred to as "demographics."

2. The sender's and receiver's likes, dislikes, hobbies, favorite TV shows, etc. This information is often called "psychographics."

3. The specific sending situation and type of card, e.g., "from mother to daughter at graduation."

4. The type of writing that is being requested (verse, prose, humor, cute, etc.).

5. The type of designs used to accompany the writing.

6. The due date. As a freelancer, the better service and faster turnaround you can give your clients, the better your chances will be for getting more assignments. (Providing, of course, your work is absolutely stellar, which it certainly should be after reading this book!)

If your needs list does not include this information, or if no needs list is available, call the editor and ask for a description of the company's consumers. (*Note*: See Chapter Fifteen—"Getting It Going, Keeping It Going"—for more on the business of greeting card writing.)

The Media

If you cannot get market information from your editor, look to the media for clues on trends and social phenomena. Analyze TV shows, movies, books, newspapers, magazines, music and art. What are people doing and saying and feeling and wearing and listening to and liking and loving and hating in the culture of today?

Hallmark's creative writing department is well stocked with dozens of the latest periodicals and newspapers. Professional writers need to read in order to keep themselves informed and stimulated.

The Industry

As a freelance social expression writer, one of your regular duties should be getting out into the marketplace—card shops, gift shops, etc.—and seeing what is going on with cards and specialty products. What's new? What's popular? What seems to be selling? Watch for which kinds of things other people shop for and buy. Keep an eye open for what might be the latest trends. Stores usually put the newer merchandise they think will sell near the front.

Interviewing store owners, too, can be valuable. Some card companies require creative and marketing executives to spend time working in card shops to observe the retail setting firsthand.

One new trend you can observe in card shops is the growing presence of "kinder, gentler" greeting cards and the peaking of caustic humor. If you can find a wonderful new way to be kind and gentle with your writing, you could sell some cards!

You

Learn to trust your own feelings. In writing to the mass market, your feelings, thoughts, ideas, likes and dislikes can be just as valuable and accurate as anyone else's. If you see an anti-yuppie, back-to-the-sixties trend coming down the road, reflect that in your writing. There's a good chance you'll be right.

Here's how to tap into your own natural social expression writing instincts:

Empathize With the Buyer/Sender

If someone asked me what is the most important attribute of a good greeting card writer, I'd say it's the ability to empathize.

Webster's says empathy is "the action of understanding, being aware of, being sensitive to, and vicariously experiencing feelings, thoughts, and experiences of another . . . without having the feelings, thoughts, and experiences fully communicated in an objectively explicit manner."

I think *Webster's* has done a pretty good job here. Empathy, for a greeting card writer, is the ability to enter the mind—and the heart—of the consumer through the doorway of imagination.

Understand the Receiver

Try to imagine who the receiver is through the feelings and perceptions of the sender. The sender wants a card to send to one particular person for one very specific reason. What does the sender think the receiver wants to hear? What does the sender think will brighten the receiver's day?

Make an Idea Sheet

While you're in a state of empathy engendered by steps one and two, jot down some feelings and ideas you think the sender would want to communicate to the receiver—not actual writing, just the raw thoughts or ideas.

EXAMPLE: You're writing a college graduation card for a mother to send to her daughter. Empathize with the mother. Say to yourself, "I *am* that mother. I have a daughter I've raised for twenty-plus years. She's graduating from college. What are my feelings?" Then jot down words like: pride, proud of you, will miss you, time flies, great kid, great times, memories, future, graduation present, moving out of house, good luck, used to wear my clothes, seem more like a friend, cap and gown, diploma, grew up too fast, bursting with pride, apartment, job hunting, seems like yesterday, world is yours.

Got the idea? You keep going until it seems most of your feelings are out and on the page. As you can see, we're starting to get very close to actual writing. And that comes now.

DOING THE WRITING

First, remain in your empathy mode, e.g., continue to be the mother of that young graduate. Then, begin looking at the ideas on your sheet and let them spark your imagination into saying, in some kind of clever or memorable or unique new way, the things you want your daughter to hear. (New writers need to write down just about everything that comes to mind. More experienced writers have the ability to edit themselves in their minds, so they'll usually be only jotting down the real zingers.) Either way, when you get something you like, write it down. Now you are writing!

I'm going to try to open up my mind and let you peer in so you can get an idea of how the wheels actually turn. (Assuming, of course, that this is one of those days when they *do* turn.) I'll pick a couple of ideas from our idea list and start building on them.

I've underlined the writing that I think might be usable.

HINT: Robert Frost defined creativity as "a feat of association." Every word or idea has a "wheel" of associated words or ideas around it. Jumping from wheel to wheel and making associations is as close as I can get to describing the actual process.

IDEA: Pride/proud. *I'm so proud* . . . how proud am I? *I'm bursting with pride* . . . what things burst? . . . balloons? . . . balloons bursting with words coming out . . . "pride" coming out? . . . the word "pride" . . . what rhymes with "pride"? (a rhyming dictionary is a must for greeting card writers) . . . hide . . . can't hide my pride . . . bursting at the seams . . . *It seems I'm bursting at the seams . . . I'm so proud I can hardly contain myself* . . . proud as a peacock (might work better from dad) . . . pride and joy . . . (this idea wants to go humorous).

Let's try another!

IDEA: Seem more like a friend. *You've always been a terrific daughter . . . over the years, you've become a terrific friend.* (Nice, but needs congrats) . . . Mom/best friend . . . *Congratulations from BOTH of us . . . your mom and your best friend!* (Design would be only one mom-type person) Too tricky? *As a daughter you've been more like a friend. As a mom, I've never been more proud!*

Get the idea? This is all very basic, but it's about as close as I can take you to give you the feeling of what is actually going on in the writer's mind. We'll be covering the different styles and forms of writing in later chapters, but you'll use this creative technique, or something similar, in all the social expression writing you do.

EMPATHY

We've spoken about it before, but it's hard to say too much about empathy. It is one of the most essential tools a greeting card writer must have. *Webster's* says, "vicarious emotion, insight, understanding." I say, it's more than that. It's a change of identity.

Social expression writers spend their workdays "being" other people. You may begin one day as a caring friend helping someone through a difficult time. After your coffee break you could become a jilted lover. Lunchtime might find you teasing a friend about being over the hill. Around 3:00 it may be time to write some fun and happiness into that clown on the unicycle for a child's fourth birthday.

All this "persona jumping" can take its toll on a writer's psyche.

One other little tip for the male writers out there: Since well over 90 percent of greeting card purchasers and senders are female, I suggest you write the following words on a three-by-five-inch card and tape it to a prominent place near your work area:

"Except when otherwise noted, I am a woman!"

It couldn't hurt — I don't think.

SENDABILITY

Don't gloss over this section. If you can figure out what I'm talking about, it can save you thousands of hours of fruitless labor and be worth thousands more dollars to your income.

"Sendability" is one of the most frequently used words and concepts in the social expression industry. It can be the single most important factor in determining whether a card (or other product) will sell.

Editors and approval committees talk about sendability all the time. Your freelance work will be screened by these people, so make sendability part of your vocabulary, too.

Sendability is the attribute of a card or other product that makes it buyable and sendable. Broad sendability means many people can buy and send it. Limited sendability means fewer people can. (The word "giftability" refers to the broadness of other social expression products' appeal.)

A card could have an artistic masterpiece on its cover, but if the message was too limiting, it would not be sendable. Similarly, a card could have a mediocre or even ugly design on its cover, and if the words were sendable heart-stoppers, it could become a best-seller.

What's the most broadly sendable card in the world? Probably one with no design and the word, "Hi!" Why? There are no flowers that might make it feminine. There's no cartoon situation to make it humorous. It doesn't say "Happy Birthday," so it can be sent to anyone, anytime. There's no reference to holiday wishes or any allusion to the personality or gender of the receiver. So what you've got here is a card that could be sent by anyone to anyone at anytime for any reason. What you've also got is the world's most boring greeting card. It's so sendable, there's nothing to it. (Okay, put a cute teddy bear holding a balloon on the cover, and you've got a million-seller!)

The best way to tell you everything you need to know about sendability is to tell you about the things that *limit* it. (Please don't get the idea that limited sendability is necessarily bad. Being specific—excluding some consumers—can also be a plus.)

EXAMPLE: If you want to write a card to a sister on her birthday, it's not a bad idea to limit it by referring to "sister" or "sis" on the front. People tend to like cards that are more specific and "just for them." Good editors and writers walk the line between "specific enough," which gives the card a strong "just-for-me" appeal, and "too specific," which will exclude too many potential purchasers.

Things That Limit Sendability

Tone or Style

Creative writing teachers spend a lot of time talking about tone and style (as they should). Tone and style in greeting card writing are equally important. But while a novelist or poet may become known for a certain style of writing, a successful social expression writer will have many styles and tones available to him or her. (Formal, informal, humorous, traditional, conversational, colloquial, satirical, etc.) The broader your versatility, the better your chance of selling your writing.

Many times your editor will suggest the tone (casual vs. formal, lighthearted vs. serious), but often you'll have the option. When you write to a specific design (as is often the case once you get established), it's important to match the tone of the writing with the tone of the design. A formal discourse on the joys of maturity does not work with a humorous design of a scraggly over-the-hill character.

Once you get your empathy skills working, tone and style should become instinctive. You'll avoid writing humor or satire when comforting a friend who's going through a rough time.

Pronouns

The important ones here are "I" vs. "we" vs. no pronoun at all.

Unless otherwise indicated, most editors like writers to keep the "I-ness" or "we-ness" out of their social expression writing. This ambiguity makes a card or product suitable for purchase by one person, a couple or a group.

Next time you browse a card rack, notice how many cards lack "I" or "we" in the writing. They'll say things like:

> (OUTSIDE): Heard another birthday cake was headed
> your way.
> (INSIDE): Hope the candles don't set off the sprinkler
> system!

Either sentence could have started with "I" or "we," but this way the card still communicates and retains its sendability.

Of course, the use of "I" is sometimes preferable (romantic love, close friendship cards), and there are times when "we" makes more sense ("We wish you a Merry Christmas"). In wedding and anniversary writing, you may also want to specify the recipient with a "you both" message.

Let the rule be: When in doubt, ask your editor.

If still in doubt, leave it out.

Descriptive Words

Be careful with adjectives and superlatives. Often senders want to pay the receiver a compliment of some kind. But remember, not everyone is pretty or smart or strong or caring or funny. Think of less limiting adjectives, such as wonderful, special, thoughtful or fun.

In family situations, use caution when comparing. It's okay to write a card for "the most wonderful mom," but not as many moms would purchase a card to "my favorite daughter."

When choosing complimentary words, consider how they might limit sendability and use the ones most broadly applicable.

Esoterica

This includes slang, regional terms, intellectualisms, etc. One thing I've learned from my years in the industry is that most people in the marketplace like writing that is simple, natural and honest. A Texan might understand what is meant by "giving someone sugar" on Valentine's Day, but a card buyer in Maine or North Dakota might think it refers to the white, granulated stuff. And bumper stickers such as "Eschew Obfuscation," while amusing, have limited appeal and staying power.

This is not to say you should disregard all fads and trends that appear in society. These can be a great resource for new ideas. Just think how many people capitalized on the classic "Where's the beef?" campaign or on the ET craze.

We'll talk more about getting ideas from trends later in the book.

Personal Nouns

Watch what you call people. Mother, Mom, Mommy, Father, Dad, Daddy, Grandmother, Grandma, Grandfather, Grandpa, Nana, Pappy, Sister, Sis, Brother, Bro, Uncle, Aunt, Auntie, etc. Some names are more limiting than others. Note the difference in these two lines:

> Mom, you are wonderful . . .
> and
> You're a wonderful Ma . . .

Which is more sendable? Which is stronger?

IMAGINATION AND CREATIVE TRICKS

You used your imagination and creativity when you picked up this book and asked, "What if . . . ?"

I've always felt that imagination is simply the ability to dream. And that creativity is the ability to ask, "What if?" If you can put these two abilities together, you might just discover you're a social expression writer!

Remember GIGO (garbage in, garbage out), that techno-clichéd acronym from Silicon Valley? Well, in a similar yet positive and creative way, a writer can improve his or her imagination by being exposed to as much information on a given subject as possible.

EXAMPLE: Say you're a humor writer. When you watch TV, tune in to comedy shows. Not just sitcoms, but comedy reviews and late-night fare. Subscribe to funny magazines: *National Lampoon*, *Spy*, *Mad*, *National Observer* (just kidding!). Go to funny movies and comedy clubs. In general, expose yourself to a wide range of funny stuff in the world.

However—and this is important—this does not mean you should use these ideas and jokes verbatim in your writing (though some writers do). What you're doing is putting this big data bank of humorous stuff into your subconscious and hoping it will resurface in new, unusual ways when you're creating your own original ideas.

It's probably presumptuous of me to try to cover the whole topic of creativity in a couple of paragraphs, when dozens of books out there are dedicated to nothing but creativity: how to get it, how to do it, right brain, left brain, meditate, cogitate, etc.

One school of thought says only the "chosen few" are blessed with creativity; either you have it or you don't.

I don't subscribe to that theory. I believe that each of us has the potential to create, whether our "medium" is numbers, machinery, paintings or greeting cards.

The following are some creative tricks to get the juices going as you begin generating ideas and concepts.

Again, there have been books written on this—*A Whack on the Side of the Head*, by Roger von Oech, published by Warner Books, is a good one.

If you've been creating for a while, you've probably already developed your own bag of tricks. If you're new at it, you'll probably invent some that will work for you as you go. Here are some techniques that have served me well over the years:

"What If . . . ?"

You could make a good argument that the ability of a person to keep saying, "What if . . ." is at the root of all creativity. Einstein said, "The important thing is not to stop questioning." And "What if . . . ?" is usually the question that will start the creative ball rolling.

EXAMPLE: Let's say you've made an idea sheet for a humorous birthday card to be sent from one woman to another. One of the words you listed was "chocolate." Your "What if . . . ?" questions might run something like this:

☛ What if the sender was made of chocolate?

☛ What if the world was made of chocolate?

☛ What if all chocolate disappeared?

☛ What if the greeting card was chocolate?

☛ What if chocolate could talk?

☛ What if chocolate came in different colors?

☛ What if there was chocolate champagne?

See? We're just setting our minds free and seeing some possibilities. Some actual writing might come out of it:

"If chocolate came in different colors, I'd send you a rainbow today." Or, you might get some design ideas out of it, e.g., humorous artwork of a champagne glass full of "chocolate champagne" with this possible copy: "They've invented the perfect birthday drink—chocolate champagne!" Or, "Here's the perfect birthday toast to a real chocolate lover!"

You could keep writing ideas on this "What if . . . ?" until you had four or five you liked and then go on to the next "What if . . . ?"

Or, you could go back to your idea sheet and "What if . . . ?" on another idea.

Allegory, Metaphor and Simile

These are usually techniques used in creative writing, but I find them useful in idea generation, too.

Here are some quickie definitions:

> **Allegory:** Using something to *mean* something else.
> *Example*: Using a river in a story to symbolize life.
>
> **Metaphor:** Saying something *is* something else.
> *Example*: That river *is* life.
>
> **Simile**: Saying something is *like* something else.
> *Example*: That river is *like* life.

Allegory, metaphor and simile are all forms of the same thing—seeing or thinking about one thing and its symbolism or similarity to another thing. Using these forms of comparing is another good creative trick.

Let's take the idea we used in the last exercise, chocolate, and see what we can do with it using this "trick."

- ☛ Chocolate is like life.
- ☛ Chocolate is like sex.
- ☛ Chocolate is joy.
- ☛ Chocolate is eternal.
- ☛ Chocolate is heaven.
- ☛ Chocolate is a river.
- ☛ Chocolate is an ocean.

Again, these thoughts — some of them, anyway — should generate some ideas for the writing or design of your birthday card. "If the ocean were chocolate, I'd send you a tidal wave for your birthday!" Or, spell out "S-E-X" in chocolate and say something like, "Here's a birthday card that combines your two favorite pastimes!" Or, "Happy birthday to someone who knows a good thing when they see it!" These are off the top of my head, but if you take some time, some really good cards can come from this process.

Wordplay

Wordplay — using rhymes, puns and alliteration — is another way to generate ideas.

Rhymes

Look at your idea sheet. What words rhyme with the words you've jotted down?

Birthday . . . Mirth Day. Earth Day. Girth Day. *Getting older*. . . Getting bolder. Getting colder. Getting colder shoulders. *Sex* . . . Hex. Tex. Wrecks. Convex.

Just keep playing around. You'll know when you hit on something you like.

Puns

Employing the previous trick, one might say, "Every fun pun under the sun has already been done." Not true. I've yet to see a card with a koala bear that uses a pun on the word "eucalyptus." Maybe *you* can write one! A word to the wise, though: There's something peculiar about a pun. No matter how clever or how original or how inventive it is, it almost always sounds corny to the ear. (See what I mean?)

Alliteration

I'm sure this isn't taught or written in any textbook, but somehow, at one time or another, all writers seem to have acquired the axiom, "When all else fails, use alliteration."

Alliteration is the use of words that begin with the same sound, e.g., tiger, temptress, titillation, pterodactyl.

And for some reason, alliteration usually works. "Hungry heart" sounds better than "famished heart" or "ravenous heart."

I'll swear to you there have been times when I've hit on one word I liked so much, that was just so perfect for a certain situation (the word "multitude," for example), that I've actually gone to the dictionary and looked through the entire "M" listing to find the perfect word to go with it. (With my luck, it's usually down around "myriad.")

Idea Substitution

Here's one you don't want to forget. Most humor writers use it all the time, and general writers use it frequently. Employed in certain ways, substitution can also become parody.

You'll often use substitution in conjunction with the wordplay tricks mentioned earlier.

EXAMPLE: Let's say the idea you're focusing on from your birthday idea sheet is still "chocolate." Start thinking of phrases that don't have the word "chocolate" in them but could use it as a substitute.

- ☛ Give me liberty or give me chocolate.
- ☛ A fool and his chocolate are soon parted.
- ☛ Happy chocolate to you!
- ☛ Go ahead, make my chocolate.

(These won't always make sense, but let's give it a try.)

Also, if you're working on idea words with rhymes, such as "pride," get the rhymes, think of statements with the rhyming word in it, *then* substitute.

EXAMPLE: We'll use the word pride. Side. Wide. Bride. Fried. Guide. Ride. Tied. Tried.

Phrase: Go along for the ride.

Changes to: Go along for the pride.

Some writers keep an ongoing list of popular phrases that they refer to and parody in this way.

Setting Limits

Nothing annoys humor writers (myself included) more than having someone find out what you do and then issue this mean-spirited challenge: "Oh, yeah? Say something funny!" I don't know about anyone else, but I could never think of a very witty comeback. One day I realized why. There are no limits to that request. It's like someone saying, "Write me a card!" I'm stumped. I need to know more. I need some limits.

If our antagonist in the previous paragraph had only said, "Oh, yeah? Say something funny about my bald spot!" Or, "Oh, yeah? Say something funny about how old I am!" I might have been able to come up with something.

So when you're stuck, it sometimes works to think smaller instead of larger, tighter instead of looser.

EXAMPLE: You're stuck trying to write a card to some friends simply thanking them for being themselves. Here are some ways you can impose limits on yourself:

Design Ideas

Think of general designs or things that might mean "thanks": a smiley face, a sunrise, a thumbs-up sign, a rabbit coming out of a hat.

Length, Style or Tone

If the assignment is wide open and your editor hasn't set limits for you here, you might find it helpful to do so for yourself. Try a four-line poem on the outside. Try something romantic-sounding. Try a definition ("What is a friend? . . ."). Try something long, rambling and stream-of-consciousness.

Time

Sometimes you get mired down in too much thinking; you suddenly realize you've been staring at your typewriter or CRT for more than an hour. "Goose" yourself by setting an arbitrary time limit. For example, say, "In the next ten minutes I'm going to write five cards, whether they're good or not." Then try five more in the next ten minutes. One or two more of these forced writing sessions and you'll either have something good, or you'll be ready to call it a day (which will also be good).

Flip-Flopping

A wise man once said, "When the front door of a house is locked, it is a good idea to go around to the back door to see if that is open." Sounds pretty obvious.

But a lot of creative people, myself included, keep banging at that front door for all it's worth because we're sure if we're clever enough and hit it in just the right place, it'll open.

You may have heard about the person who invented Velcro because he noticed how burrs stuck to his pants when he walked through the undergrowth. Or the scientist at 3M who came up with Post-it notes because he needed something to mark his place in his choir book.

That kind of free-form, divergent thinking is one of the real cornerstones of the creative process.

So when you're stuck on something, go around to the back door. Think opposites.

What *isn't* chocolate? What *isn't* friendship? What's the furthest thing from a smiley face? Who *don't* you love? When is a cat *not* a cat?

And most important, keep that mind moving and jumping around. Even if the back door's locked, there's usually an open window somewhere. *Tip*: You might copy down the headings of the "Tricks" sections on a three-by-five-inch card and display them as reminders.

PART
TWO

Traditional
Greeting
Cards

CHAPTER THREE

It Takes All Kinds of Cards

Most companies divide greeting cards into two major categories: everyday cards (cards that may be sold year-round) and seasonal cards. There are quite a few kinds in both categories, so I'll take you through all of them, starting with types in the "everyday" category. First, I'll tell you everything I know about all the particular seasons or events, and then talk about the kinds of writing in each that I've had the most success with.

This chapter will be helpful when you get specific assignments. You can simply look up the section on the type of cards you're writing and refresh your memory.

What Is a Greeting Card Caption?

In this chapter and those that follow, I'll use the word *caption* quite extensively. To the world at large, a caption usually means the words that go under a cartoon or photograph. In the world of greeting cards, it takes on an additional meaning. Here it is used to define or identify a particular type of card, a group of cards, or a particular sending situation.

EXAMPLE: *Birthday* is a caption. *Missing you* is a caption. *Christmas/sister and husband*, too.

Let's say your editor (or your client) asks for humorous birthday cards. You would need to ask, "Which captions are you looking for?"

The editor might respond, "We've got plenty of 'age slams.' What we need is 'age compliment,' and 'female-to-female shared experience.' " (These captions are explained in chapters Nine and Eleven.)

Once you know which captions are in demand, you can direct all your energies toward those and not waste your time working on stuff they don't need.

Everyday Cards

As already stated, everyday cards are the cards that are in the store year-round. By definition, they address a particular event or happening in the life of the receiver, rather than a seasonal event or holiday.

By far the most popular everyday card-sending event is *birthday*.

Other specific personal events that fall on certain days every year would be *wedding* and *anniversary*.

Other everyday cards address noncalendar-specific occasions, such as *get well*, *sympathy* and *new baby*; and some others are meant for all-occasion sending, such as *friendship* and *missing you*.

A Note About Line Balance

Greeting card editors try very hard to create a balanced line of cards. They accomplish this by providing a variety of messages, ideally something for everyone, in the group of cards they plan. For this reason, editors often are very specific in the types of writing they request.

The following are only a few of the aspects of card writing editors must balance within greeting card lines:

- Length of copy
- Tone of copy
- Prose/verse
- Humor/general
- Intimacy of copy

An editor's list of writing needs may sound arbitrary. But remember, greeting card companies may choose from many messages they have on file. When an editor requests short prose, you won't have much luck selling long verse. Write what they're looking for, and you'll sell more cards.

We'll now walk through all the everyday captions and learn about the very specific types of cards you might be asked to write to help an editor create an editorially balanced line.

SPECIFIC OCCASIONS

Birthday

Because birthday is the biggest everyday card sending occasion, we'll look at it in the most detail. Editors need a wide variety of messages when editing or putting together a birthday line. General birthday cards can be sent from anyone to anyone. They contain no specific information (age, relationship, gender, etc.) about the recipient. General birthday cards are divided into captions by the *type* of wish or message contained in the card. (The terminology and delineation of these types of messages varies from company to company. For simplicity's sake, I have divided the cards into three groups: *general wish*, *compliments* and *close relationship*.) Editors may want specific categories, so pay attention!

General Wish

This is pretty self-explanatory—the card contains only a wish. Not a compliment. Not *love*. A wish. Period.

The wishes can range from very cool and tailored ("Many happy returns on your birthday") to very warm and effusive ("Wishing you the moon, the sea, the stars, and everything you've ever dreamed of").

General wish cards can be either verse or prose, humorous or serious.

Because a simple wish does not say anything specific about the relationship between the sender and the recipient, general wish cards are the most sendable and least limiting of all birthday cards.

Compliments

A compliment birthday card goes one step further than wishing the recipient a happy birthday. It says something like, "You're a nice/sweet/special/thoughtful/wonderful/swell/sexy/whatever person."

Like wishes, compliments can range from cool and reserved (as in the implied compliment, "Wishing you all the happiness you deserve") to downright embarrassing ("You're a big bundle of cuteness and spunk").

Compliment cards are appropriate for relationships on many levels of intimacy. The same nice compliment card might be appropriate for a co-worker, neighbor, baby-sitter, son or grandmother.

That's the beauty of writing compliment cards. You have the opportunity to say something really nice to someone without getting too intensely personal. But if your editor *needs* some writing that's intensely personal, you might be asked to write the next type of birthday card.

Close Relationship

Close relationship cards deal in feelings—feelings that might include love, pride, respect, awe, gratitude, friendship, devotion, guilt, lust, or any other emotion that could exist between a sender and receiver.

Here are some examples of compliment and close relationship birthday wishes. Notice the difference in "point of view" between the two types:

COMPLIMENT	CLOSE RELATIONSHIP
You're an extraordinary person.	You've changed my life.
You're pretty sexy.	I want your body.
You're a loving person.	Thank you for loving me.
You've achieved some important goals.	I'm really proud of you.

I'm sure you get the idea. Although the message is similar in all of the pairs of card ideas, the one on the left could be sent by almost anyone to almost anyone. The close relationship cards on the right, though, suggest much more intimacy between the sender and receiver.

As you shall see, these three categories—general wish, compliment and close relationship—apply also to cards in many other captions, both everyday and seasonal.

Miscellaneous or Special Birthday

Also included in the general birthday category are some odd captions—*belated, across the miles, from all, from both* and *age-specific* (fortieth, fiftieth, etc.). The freelance opportunity here is minimal, with the exception of belated birthday.

In belated birthday, it's best to keep your apologies and excuses light-hearted but sincere. (We'll discuss belated and age-specific birthdays in Chapter Nine, "How to Write Traditional Humor.")

Relative Birthday

Birthday cards for relatives are cleverly divided into two major groups: masculine and feminine. *Dad, son, brother, brother-in-law, grandfather, grandson, uncle,* and *nephew* are the main masculine birthday captions. *Mom, daughter, sister, sister-in-law, grandmother, granddaughter, aunt* and *niece* are the main feminine categories.

Let your common sense rule when writing cards for relatives. In general, editors look for cards in the feminine captions to be warmer and more intimate than those in the masculine. As you might expect, masculine captions permit you to write more caustic humor and fewer mushy feelings. (Chapters Nine and Eleven, dealing with traditional and alternative humor, will address relative-bashing in greater detail.)

Editors look for sincerity and newness in writing for relatives. The following are some fairly obvious hints for the specific relative captions:

Mom or dad cards might mention memories, home/family, sacrifices made, parent as friend, thanks for everything and respect.

Grandparent cards might include feelings of respect, memories of grandparents' times, thanks for wisdom, compliments and gratitude.

Brother and sister cards are natural places to write about sharing, growing up together, friendship and love.

(*Note*: Juvenile birthday cards are covered in Chapter Seven.)

Wedding

Romanticism is alive and well on wedding cards, and it's the perfect opportunity for all you old softies to strut your stuff.

There is a wedding card market for traditional verse and inspirational prose, as well as cute and whimsical copy. Religious wedding cards also are a good bet.

Write about dreams coming true, promises being made, wedding imagery, and the future. Be idealistic and effusive about the power of love. Compliments to the couple are appropriate, as are wishes for happiness together.

Anniversary

The writing for anniversary cards can be less traditional than that for wedding wishes. (Chapter Nine will give you hints on writing humorous anniversary cards.)

The three major categories within the anniversary caption are *wedding anniversary*, *our wedding anniversary*, and *general anniversary*.

Wedding Anniversary

Obviously, these are cards written for one or more people to send to a couple celebrating their anniversary.

Good wedding anniversary copy refers to memories, congratulations, celebrations, love (of course!) and yesterday/today/tomorrow. Nostalgic imagery also is a marketable approach. Your writing may compliment the celebrating couple on either their personal attributes or on the wonderful marriage they appear to have.

Our Wedding Anniversary

These cards are sent by spouse to spouse in celebration of their anniversary. They need to be more warm and intimate than cards to the couple from friends and family.

Include close relationship feelings such as love, pride, gratitude and friendship, as well as references to the many memories the couple has shared through the years.

General Anniversary

These cards are intended for people celebrating anniversaries other than wedding. You can assume that people celebrating business or professional anniversaries will receive the majority of these cards.

Consequently, general anniversary cards tend to be either very tailored (in both design and copy) or light and humorous.

Some good general anniversary words and phrases include *hard work, dedication, occasion, congratulations* and *best wishes*. Light compliments also work well. Keep your wishes general, because this is usually a small caption; therefore editors like to keep the cards as sendable as possible.

Retirement

Retirement is a very significant life occasion in our society. Editors look both for worker-to-worker cards and family/friends-to-worker cards in this caption. Avoid suggesting that all a retiree has to look forward to is going fishing or doing needlework.

More Americans are staying healthy, living longer, and keeping active than ever before. The "mature" market is getting larger and more powerful every year, and editors look for writing to hit that market in a new and better way.

Not many people, no matter *how* old they are, really think of themselves as being old. So remember, when you're writing retirement cards—or any cards that address the mature market—*don't patronize*.

Show respect. Imagine yourself being that age, but *feeling* the way you do right now. (Providing you're younger, of course. If you're older, you already know what I'm talking about.)

Some good words and phrases to start with in writing retirement cards are *take it easy*, *your own boss*, *memories*, *dreams*, *dedication*, *hard work*, and, of course, *congratulations*.

Light and humorous retirement cards are appropriate, as are inspirational messages. Just make sure any humor is complimentary and upbeat.

Remember, many retirees are as sharp and as hip as you are (maybe even more), so whatever you do, don't pander or "write down" to them. Treat them as the equals that they are. And give them respect—they've earned it!

NONSPECIFIC OCCASIONS

There are many unplanned occasions when people are prompted to send a card. If I happen to miss some that you think of, please forgive me for being human, and give yourself a pat on the back for being sharp!

Cheer

When someone is sick, has an accident, is hospitalized, has an operation, or stubs a toe on the piano, people send a cheer card. Editors look for three basic types of cards within the cheer caption: *get well*, *hospital* and *thinking of you*.

Once again, common sense should dictate the tone and content of your cheery copy.

Get Well

These are the least serious-minded of the cheer cards. The assumption that the mildly ill recipient will, indeed, get well allows the writer to be lighthearted, humorous or friendly. Some get-well words and phrases are *recovery*, *feeling better*, *healthier days ahead*, and *sorry you're sick*.

Hospital

When someone is in the hospital for a minor operation, you can kid around. But when someone is seriously ill, you need to take a more sensitive approach. Editors need both types of writing in this caption.

Some good hospital phrases are *get some rest*, *those darn nurses*, *how's the food?*, *hope you're comfortable*, and *hurry home*.

Thinking of You

This cheer caption is the trickiest to write. Editors look for cards with an uplifting, cheerful message, suitable to send to anyone needing cheering up for any reason. A great demand exists for suitable cards to send to people in rest homes and nursing homes, as well as to those who are terminally ill.

Some good thinking-of-you phrases are *in my thoughts*, *quiet moments*, *warmest thoughts*, *never far from thought*, *comfort*, *peace*, *blessings*, *take care*, and *God's care*.

Sympathy

Editors look for sympathy writing in two basic categories: *general* and *religious/inspirational*.

Some inexperienced writers have a sense of inadequacy when trying to write sympathy cards. After all, what are the right words to say to a grieving person? But if you keep your writing honest, sensitive and caring, you may be able to share a thought or feeling that might really help someone.

Some strong sympathy messages are *I'm sorry this happened*, *I'm thinking about you*, *I care about you*, *I'm here if you need me*, *may your memories comfort you*, and *know that loving thoughts are with you*.

Avoid presuming to know how the bereaved person feels. Don't preach.

There is always a need for strong, inspirational quotes for the cover of sympathy cards. Visit the sympathy section of a card shop and you'll see what I mean.

Thank You

Thank you is a fairly small caption, but editors occasionally need fresh, new copy. The tone of a thank-you card can range from humorous to effusive. It's a natural format for complimenting the thoughtfulness and generosity of the recipient, as well as for declaring the indebtedness of the sender.

General Congratulations

There are times in peoples' lives when they deserve (and sometimes get) congratulations. Some of these reasons are: promotions in the workplace; achievement of a specific goal, such as dieting and quitting smoking; and buying a new car or house.

This, too, is a fairly small caption. But just in case you have reason to write for it, some good congratulatory words and phrases are *achievement*, *well-deserved success*, *nice going*, *pride*, and *rah-rah-rah!*

Baby Congrats

There is almost no way you can overdramatize, over-recognize or over-cutesify the birth of a baby. And rightly so. There is nothing more dramatic (to new parents, anyway). And absolutely nothing cuter in the world. Pull out all the stops. Let it rip.

If you're beginning to see the pattern in greeting card captions, you've no doubt guessed that baby congrats is divided into *baby boy*, *baby girl* and *general* (suitable for boy or girl). The baby congrats line also includes miniscule captions such as *twins*, *new grandchild*, *baptism* and *mother-to-be*.

Some good words and phrases for new baby cards are *precious*, *dream come true*, *little one*, *treasure*, *goo-goo*, *bottle*, *bibs*, *blankies*, *love*, *cherish*, *bundle*, *hugs* and *kisses*.

Complimenting the new parents also works well.

Miscellaneous Friendship

Friendship cards are referred to as "all occasion," and they are divided into four categories: *friend*, *hello*, *thinking of you*, and *missing you*.

(*Note*: There is also a new type of alternative card called "non-occasion." This is covered in chapter ten.)

"All-occasion" cards are an ongoing need for greeting card editors. Chapters Nine and Eleven deal with humorous all-occasion writing.

General all-occasion writing has a light, warmhearted tone. Some idea-starting words include *friend*, *sharing*, *confide*, *warm thoughts*, *memories*, *missing you*, *times together*, *closeness*, *relationship*, and *keep in touch*.

SEASONAL CARDS

Before you begin writing and selling seasonal cards, be sure to find out which season your editor or client is working on at that particular time. Generally, an editor does not have the energy to look at Halloween copy, no matter how wonderful, while in the throes of planning a Christmas line. (Everyday cards are usually purchased on an ongoing basis; seasonal cards are not.)

If you look at a calendar, you will notice at least one "greeting card holiday" per month, with the exception of August. I will start with January and cover the greeting card seasons throughout the year.

New Year's Day

Because most wishes for a "Happy New Year" have already been tendered in Christmas greetings, New Year's is a small season. However, for specialty (noncard) products, New Year's is more important.

One word of advice on writing copy for New Year's cards or specialty products: Getting drunk isn't as funny as it used to be. Our society has realized that this formerly fun and festive, wild-and-crazy activity can have disastrous, life-damaging consequences.

So, while it's probably still okay to tell people to "party down" and "celebrate your buns off," cards that encourage or mention excessive drinking and drunkenness won't sell nearly as well as they used to. (See "Graduation," pages 42-44.)

Valentine's Day

Everybody knows that this is the season of love. And except for Christmas, Valentine's Day is the top-selling greeting card season of the year.

The demand for Valentine writing includes a fun variety of feelings and messages. Valentines are sent not only from sweetheart to sweetheart, but from friend to friend, from parent to child, and from relative to relative. For simplicity, I'll divide the Valentine writing tips into two categories: romantic and nonromantic.

37

Romantic Valentines

Let's talk about love. What is it? Where do you find it? When you find it, how do you get it? How do you make it stay?

Thank goodness for greeting cards, right? They've made it a lot easier for you to take a chance and tell that certain someone what you're feeling. You don't have to write it in some serious-sounding letter or, worse yet, say it in person.

Romantic Valentine writing falls into three easily managed pieces: *early, new or growing relationship*; *established relationship*; and *relationship in trouble*.

1. Early, new or growing relationship. There's a lot of this going around. Valentines for this sending situation are very marketable. People who buy and send cards tend to buy and send a *lot* of cards at this particular time in their lives. The copy can range from cautious to suggestive to downright passionate during the growing part of the relationship.

Some good words and phrases for new-love Valentines are *beginnings, new, exciting, hopeful, taking risks, be my whatever*, and *hot sex*. (You *do* remember what it feels like, don't you?)

Actually, the current trend is for editors to avoid the blatantly sexual cards that made it into the marketplace ten or fifteen years ago. You remember these cards — the ones with naked people and dirty words that were purchased, if at all, solely for the shock value.

If you *are* writing something overtly suggestive, be sure that there's a good idea supporting it. Gratuitous sex has its place — but not on greeting cards!

2. Established relationships. They say the best relationships are the ones that are always growing. It's fun to write cards for lovers who've been together for a while. There's a certain honesty and earthiness in established relationships, and those qualities are easier for most of us to relate to than hearts and flowers.

Remember that what established relationships may lack in fervor and immediacy, they make up for in intimacy, trust, gratitude and friendship. And don't be afraid to add the passion, too!

Some good established-relationship Valentine ideas are *comfortable, contented, secure, trusting, memories, when the kids are asleep, our special times together, thank you*, and *you're my best friend*.

3. Relationships in trouble. These cards aren't too numerous, but

this type of message allows a writer to try some innovative ideas for difficult situations.

Some difficult-times Valentine messages include *I'm sorry, I miss having you as my Valentine, I'm glad we're still friends*, and *can't we still be friends?*

Nonromantic Valentines

Nonromantic Valentines can be divided into three major categories: *relatives, juvenile* and *friendship*.

1. Relatives. Writing and selling Valentines for relatives is very similar to writing birthday cards for relatives, and the hints and information in the birthday section should be helpful to aspiring Valentine writers. Naturally, editors expect more emphasis on love in Valentines, however.

2. Juvenile. Chapter Seven will give you specific writing tips for *all* juvenile cards, but remember that Valentine's Day is a big juvenile season because of the packaged cards kids exchange at school. Licensed properties (whatever Saturday morning cartoon characters are currently popular) are good subject matter for packaged Valentines. Riddles, puns and "knock-knock" jokes are among editors' other favorites.

3. Friendship. Valentines for friends can have several different tones and purposes. One marketable approach is a sincere declaration of feelings of a woman's friendship toward a friend of either sex. For example:

> "On Valentine's Day, I'd just like to say,
> It's nice to have a friend like you!"

As a writer, it's your job to think of various ways to express those feelings. The writing tips in the "Miscellaneous Friendship" section of this chapter should help you.

Another way friends communicate on Valentine's Day is to help each other cope with the stress of love relationships. For example:

> "Here's hoping Cupid's been good to you this year!"
> or
> "If love makes the world go 'round, this planet's
> in trouble!"

Some of these "coping with love" cards can get rather derogatory toward men. This caustic approach is very marketable, as it appeals to the large number of working women in their twenties and thirties who buy and send a lot of greeting cards. For example, "I like men . . . it's the whiskers in the sink I can't stand!"

The third Valentine friendship category is chocolate. Here's a category that everyone—married, single, divorced or other—can identify with. For some reason, Valentine's Day really brings the chocolate lovers out of the cracks. Use it in unimaginable amounts, compare it to love, equate it with sex, make other objects out of it.

For example:

> "Chocolate is better than a man because chocolate doesn't mess up your transmission when it drives your car!"
>
> or
>
> "May your Valentine's Day be filled with love, music, sunshine, and a five-pound box of chocolate fudge truffles!"

St. Patrick's Day

Even though this is the nineties, I'm sure some companies will still pay for St. Patrick's Day cards that use excessive drinking and ethnic put-downs as their themes. That's their business if they want to pay for them and, quite honestly, your business if you want to write them. Most editors, though, are looking for St. Patrick's Day ideas that don't reduce anyone to a cultural stereotype.

These cards can range in tone from serious to cute to funny. The St. Patrick's Day Idea Starter in the Workbook section will get you going.

Easter

This is the first religious season we'll discuss. As you probably know, in the Christian culture, Easter is the time of resurrection, of rebirth, of new life, of rejoicing. It is a happy coincidence that in the northern hemisphere, this holiday often coincides with the coming of spring, a natural event that has similar joyous connotations.

Editors look for both religious and secular copy for Easter.

Religious and inspirational writing are discussed in more detail in Chapter Six, but note that resurrection themes such as He is risen, Rejoice, and Hallelujah, are strongest for this season.

Keep in mind that several companies, such as Dayspring, publish *only* religious cards. Also remember the "new-Christian" market, for which you can try writing some religious cards with an updated, conversational tone. As always, looking at some current cards will help you learn what kinds of language and design are being used.

Secular Easter cards tend to celebrate nature, new beginnings and springtime in a lighthearted and joyful way.

"Happy Easter, Happy Spring!" with a cute, fuzzy baby chick on the cover is a good example. Juvenile cards for Easter rely quite heavily on the Easter Bunny, eggs, candy, and the surprises that will be forthcoming.

Humorous cards at Easter are in a minority, but editors have purchased ideas involving Easter candy, the Easter Bunny, Easter grass and marshmallow chicks (ugh!).

Mother's Day

The third most popular greeting card season, right under Christmas (huge) and Valentine's Day (very large), is Mother's Day. And as with Valentine's Day, it is emotion-filled.

"There is no one like a mother . . ." is the beginning message on many of the cards. And at Mother's Day, there is nothing like a card to tell her so.

These cards will carry the whole gamut of writing styles and designs, but one thing is very important, and you must never forget it: *Don't make fun of your mother!*

Mother's Day cards should be nice to Mom and tell her how much she means to you, even if you don't always remember to tell her so in person. (The "mother birthday" writing tips on page 32 should be helpful to you in writing Mother's Day cards.)

For some reason, Father's Day cards can tease Dad quite a bit (as you'll see). But there seems to be something deeper—almost sacred—about the mother relationship that doesn't leave much room for the teasing style you can use for Father's Day.

So when you want to write funny things to Mom, you'll focus on how you used to wear her clothes, or how messy your room was, or what a chore it must have been to raise someone like you, or how she was always there to kiss the boo-boos. Specific images of childhood and family times help make a Mother's Day idea unique and marketable.

(Hi, Mom!)

Father's Day

On the other hand, there's Dad. Good ol' Dad. . . .

In general writing, it is often harder to express deep, more intimate feelings to Dad than it is to Mom. (See "dad birthday" writing tips, page 32.) I think this might be because men have not been socialized to express intimate feelings. (How 'bout them Giants?)

Editors look for sincere, but not syrupy, compliments to Dad: *thanks for always being there*; *you showed me the way*; *you were gentle in your strength, strong in your gentleness*. Keep in mind that your writing will probably be illustrated with a photo of a lighthouse, a ship, or a duck decoy!

In the humor area, it's open season on Dad. Getting the keys to the car, Dad's weird outfits, Dad lending you money, waiting up late while you were out on dates—all of these Dad-things are the raw material from which great Father's Day cards come. (Thanks, Dad. Oh, and *nice* tie!)

Graduation

There is a market for high school, college and general graduation cards. Keep in mind that in all three types, the sending situation can be either adult-to-graduate or peer-to-graduate. If the graduate is lucky, many of the adult-to-graduate cards will contain large sums of money tucked right in there with the congratulations and wishes for good luck. Peer-to-graduate cards are from brothers, sisters and longtime friends.

Adult-to-Graduate

Whether the student is graduating from high school or college, the basic theme here is "Congratulations!"

Editors look for traditional copy that will work well with traditional graduation designs: rainbows, sea gulls soaring upward, sunrises, sailboats majestically leaving the harbor, and other inspirational scenes.

Inspirational quotations—from others or from *you*—on the cover of a card are very marketable for graduation. My favorite is Tennyson's, "Arise, go forth and conquer!" It's kind of an overstated example of what graduation writing is all about.

Write an inspiring inside for the card—"Wishing you the best in everything you do"—and you've created a whole graduation package, and quite possibly, a sale. (*Note*: Quotations are discussed in detail in Chapter Six.)

Bartlett's Familiar Quotations is an excellent source of words of wisdom to feature on your cards. It's best to make sure that your quotation is in the public domain (not protected by copyright). If it is under copyright, your editor will need to get permission to use it on a card. For specific information on copyright law, see Chapter Fifteen, "Getting It Going, Keeping It Going."

If you write your own graduation quotation, terrific. Just put your name on it and you'll be right up there alongside Shakespeare and Thoreau. The real kick comes when you find out that *your* quotation is outselling *theirs*!

Peer-to-Graduate

Editors look for both humorous and sincere friendship ideas for peer-to-graduate cards. Some good topics for graduation humor are *grades*, *teachers*, *vacation*, *the real world*, *immaturity*, *get a job*, and *party time*. (*Note*: Many editors are sensitive to the dangers of young graduates drinking and driving. When writing your graduation cards, do *not* advocate getting drunk.)

For this season, it's helpful to remember the types of people in your old school. Were they brains, party-goers, jocks, cheerleaders, jokers, nerds, hippies? What were they going to be when they "grew up"? What do you miss about them? What *don't* you miss about them?

One caution: If you're going to tease someone, whether it be brother, sister or friend, make sure there's some love underneath it. The strongest and most marketable cards avoid mean-spiritedness. If you're going to push someone a little, follow it up with a smile or a hug. Or put yourself in the joke with them, as in the following example for brother graduation:

> (OUTSIDE): Nobody who studied as little as you—and
> who partied as hard—has any business
> graduating!

(INSIDE): I guess genius just runs in our family!
Congratulations!

Grandparent's Day

Celebrated on the second Sunday of September, this holiday has been accused of being exploitive and unnecessary. I disagree.

I think that an occasion that allows us to recognize, compliment, and show respect for our elders is a welcome and positive social practice. (After all, we'll all be elders someday!)

At any rate, Grandparent's Day is still a relatively small holiday, marketwise. You'll find the cards are divided into two major segments: those to be sent by children, and those to be sent by adults.

Chapter Seven, "How to Write Great Juvenile Cards," covers child-to-adult greetings in detail. The grandmother and grandfather birthday tips in this chapter should help you get started on the adult-to-grandparent cards.

Halloween

Boo! You're about to learn how to write for one of the most fun greeting card seasons in the year. Rather amazingly, editors look for about equal numbers of good juvenile and adult copy for Halloween. I guess when it comes to Halloween, we're all just kids at heart.

Juvenile cards range from cute to benignly scary. For example:

"The Gramercy Ghost has come on the scene,
to wish you a frightfully fun Halloween."

Kids love to hear about ghosts and goblins, ghouls and vampires, witches and devils, cats and bats — and candy.

Wordplay is a great device for kids' Halloween cards:

"I vant to vish you a happy Halloveen!"

Guess what? Editors buy adult Halloween cards with many of the same themes and words:

"Happy Halloween, Snickers-Breath!"

The Halloween Idea Starter in the Workbook section will be a valuable tool as you create cards to scare the socks off your editor!

Thanksgiving

Thanksgiving cards recognize the essence of the holiday (giving thanks for the harvest), either religiously (by mentioning God) or secularly (by merely alluding to the idea of thankfulness). Editors look for warm, expansive copy that deals with family ties, togetherness, abundance and blessings. Keep it warm, honest, family-oriented and also "thankful."

There *is* some need for Thanksgiving humor writing, as well, probably because turkeys are so innately funny. And a lot of funny ideas can come from the overindulgence of the event. (I never seem to "get my fill" of drumstick jokes.) Luckily, the Thanksgiving vernacular also possesses one of the funniest words in the English language—a word so hilarious that if you merely use it at all, you're almost guaranteed an instant sale. Are you ready for the word? Here it is. The word is *giblets*.

Christmas

It's probably obvious to you that Christmas is by far the largest holiday season for greeting cards. When we speak of Christmas cards, we're really speaking of two different types of cards: boxed and individual.

When writing for either boxed or individual Christmas cards, remember the importance of Christmas imagery: candles, snowfall, carol singing, bells ringing, love and laughter, snowmen, mittens, hats, churches, sleighs. Christmas copy is the most evocative greeting card copy, and editors look for writing that captures the "old Christmas feeling" in a new and better way.

Boxed Christmas Cards

The writing on boxed Christmas cards tends to be slightly reserved and widely sendable. After all, one person is to send this same piece of copy to all his or her friends, clients and relatives. This is not to say that innovative copy has no place on boxed Christmas cards; but by and large, the adage "keep it simple" holds true.

Because so many interesting visual possibilities exist with boxed cards, you may want to suggest an innovative design idea with some fairly straightforward copy.

For example, if you started with a yellow smiley face wearing a Santa hat, the very simple "Have a nice holiday" creates a total design/editorial concept.

I should note that, in any season (as well as everyday), writers who can think visually and artists who can think editorially are the most successful creators in the social expression industry. Any time you can submit a total design and editorial package, even if the design is described and not sketched, you enhance your odds of making a sale. This especially holds true in humor.

Some companies use alternative humor on boxed cards. If you try to sell a humorous boxed card, don't cross the boundaries of good taste. Make fun of Santa, but be good-natured about it. Stay away from the religious side of Christmas. Try parodies and/or puns of traditions, songs (careful with carols), and the crass commercialization of the holiday.

Individual Christmas Cards

A writer can take more risks with individual Christmas cards than with boxed cards, because the consumer only has to buy and send that one card.

Sending situations include "love," "juvenile," "across the miles," "relatives," and many tiny captions including "to the mail carrier" and "pet-to-pet."

The relative birthday writing tips on pages 31-32 should help you write some meaningful Christmas cards for family sending situations. To create the most marketable copy, be sure to combine Christmas imagery with "close relationship" messages.

The Christmas Idea Starter in the Workbook section will help you get going on writing both general and humorous boxed cards.

Jewish Holidays

The primary market needs for Jewish seasonal cards center around four major holidays: Passover (Pesach), Rosh Hashanah, Yom Kippur and Hanukkah.

Passover

On the Lunar calendar, Passover, which celebrates the exodus of the Israelites from Egypt, falls sometime in March or April. Thus, the central theme of the Passover is liberation, freedom and new life, which is also exemplified by the natural seasonal changes from winter to spring.

Central symbols are the unleavened bread, or matzoh; the feast of the seder plate; and the eating of only kosher-for-Passover foods that week.

Cards about Passover are usually pretty traditional and almost always very uplifting and joyful.

Rosh Hashanah

This is what is known as the Jewish New Year, and the cards will have about the same sending dynamics as the January 1 New Year of the solar calendar. It's a time to reflect on the year past and give wishes for happiness, health and good fortune for the coming year. It is also the beginning of ten days of repentance, the ending of which is marked by Yom Kippur. One of the major traditions of Rosh Hashanah is the blowing of the shofar, a kind of horn that is blown several times during the festival.

Cards should be happy and lighthearted and can even verge on the humorous.

Yom Kippur

Yom Kippur, which falls nine days after Rosh Hashanah, is the day of Atonement and the end of those ten days of repentance. Yom Kippur is the most solemn day of the year. The following words and phrases give a good idea of the sort of wishes you might want to convey: Open for us the gates of light, blessing, joy, knowledge, splendor, confession, merit, compassion, purity, salvation, atonement, kindness, forgiveness, solace, pardon, assistance, sustenance, righteousness, uprightness, healing, peace and repentance.

Hanukkah

Hanukkah is known as the "festival of lights," which celebrates the victory of the Maccabees over the armies of Alexander the Great. When the Maccabees reclaimed the temple of Jerusalem and lit the menorah, there was only enough oil to burn for one day; yet the flame burned for *eight* days, thereby creating the "miracle of the oil." Thus was born the tradition of lighting one more candle each night during the time of the celebration.

Other traditions include making and playing with dreidels, which are four-sided tops with a Hebrew letter inscribed on each side.

Hanukkah is a lighthearted happy time, not nearly so solemn as some of the other Jewish holidays, which gives you the chance to write all types of warm wishes for the season. Hanukkah cards are used much in the same way as Christmas cards; in fact many Christmas cards with sentiments such as "Season's Greetings" or "Happy Holidays" serve this holiday just fine.

Whether everyday or seasonal, cards help people share the joy of special events and comfort each other in troubled times. So don't hold back. Go for the fun, the happiness, the celebration, the sympathy that make people want to reach out—with a card.

CHAPTER FOUR

"DAH-dee-DAH-dee-DAH-dee-DAH"
OR

How to Write
Traditional Verse

You may have noticed that greeting card verse writers are the Rodney Dangerfields of the literary world. As a matter of fact, in the hierarchy of writing, rhymed greeting cards probably rank somewhere between chain letters and sweepstakes notifications.

Although most people describe these "old-fashioned" cards as smarmy or contrived, someone out there (many people, in fact) keeps buying them.

I think the bad rap comes from greeting cards of the past, when artificial poetry extolled the virtues of a "grand person" or "an auntie who's dear." Actually, though, if you check out the traditional section in a card or gift shop today, you will find some very nice, stylish poetry with an interesting message and structure.

These are the three secrets of writing marketable greeting card verse: Give it structure, make it contemporary, and make it say something.

I should note that the demand for humorous one-liners is much larger than the demand for verse. Still, if you're interested in becoming a well-rounded social expression writer, the ability to write rhymed and metered sentiments is essential.

POETRY 101

The following is a crash course for all you aspiring rhymers out there. The structure of greeting card verse can be looked at as the marriage of its meter (the rhythmic pattern of stressed and unstressed syllables within each line) and its rhyme (the pattern of rhymed and unrhymed lines within each verse) to create a piece of poetry.

The Complete Rhyming Dictionary, edited by Clement Wood, is excellent for help both in studying rhyme and meter schemes and in finding rhyming words for your verses.

Meter

The rhythm of a poem (or greeting card verse) is called its "meter." Reading a poem to determine its meter is referred to as "scanning." When you scan a poem, listen for which syllables (or "beats") in each line are stressed, or accented, and which are unstressed, or unaccented.

Ī've bĕen tŏ / Lōndŏn tŏ /   two dactyls

vīsĭt thĕ / qūeen . ˘˘ /   two dactyls

A dactylic greeting card verse would be:

Wĭshĭñg yŏu / hāppĭnĕss, /   two dactyls

laūghtĕr, añd / lōve ˘   two dactyls

Ã / bīrthdăy thăt's / evĕřythĭng /   two dactyls

yoū're drĕamĭñg / ōf! ˘ ˘ /   two dactyls

Don't worry if it takes a while to learn to meter a greeting card. Give your ear lots of practice and soon you'll be picking out the meter in everything from "The Rime of the Ancient Mariner" to *Barry Manilow's Greatest Hits.*

If you can master the four meters explained above, you'll have a good repertoire of poetic tools for writing traditional verse. Careful metering takes a little extra time, but a well-metered verse sounds much more professional than a bumpy attempt at poetry. For best results, take your time and rewrite until it sounds like music!

Some editors, especially those who, themselves, are poetically inclined, are real sticklers for meter. Others will not require strict metering if the idea is fresh and strong.

Rhyme Scheme

Rhyme scheme is the pattern of rhymed and unrhymed lines within a poem. Let's take a look at this familiar rhyme to determine its rhyme scheme:

> Humpty Dumpty sat on a wall,
> Humpty Dumpty had a great fall.
> All the king's horses and all the king's men
> Couldn't put Humpty together again.

The first line (and all lines rhyming with the first line) will be labeled "A." The next line with a new rhyme (and all other lines rhyming with that line) will be labeled "B," and so on.

Here's how "Humpty Dumpty" would be labeled as a rhyme scheme:

Humpty Dumpty sat on a wall,	A
Humpty Dumpty had a great fall.	A
All the king's horses and all the king's men	B
Couldn't put Humpty together again.	B

"Humpty Dumpty" has an A-A-B-B rhyme scheme. "Wall" rhymes with "fall," and "men" rhymes with "again." When two consecutive lines of poetry rhyme, those two lines are called a "couplet." "Humpty Dumpty" consists of two couplets.

Let's try another rhyme:

Sing a song of sixpence,	A
A pocket full of rye;	B
Four-and-twenty blackbirds	C
Baked in a pie.	B

In this poem, the first line, "A," does not rhyme with the second line. So we call the second line "B." The third line rhymes with neither of the preceding lines, so we call it "C." The fourth line rhymes with the second line, so it is also labeled "B." This poem has an A-B-C-B rhyme scheme. Many greeting cards have this rhyme scheme:

A warm and loving message	A
on your special day—	B
Here's hoping lots of happiness	C
will always come your way.	B

Be advised that companies seldom will purchase such a generic greeting card verse. A verse's message and structure must set it apart from the thousands of verses already existing in editors' files.

Greeting card writers use dozens of rhyme schemes. If you are interested in writing verse greeting cards, study the rhyme schemes used by the great poets: Shakespeare, Shelley, Wordsworth, Frost. Adapt them to specific card-sending situations. Study greeting cards, too. Some very touching images and thoughts are communicated with interesting structures and rhymes in today's verse cards.

Rhyming Words

Certain words are hackneyed "greeting card words," and although they make great *rhymes*, they make lousy *messages*. Avoid the following rhyme words, if possible:

☛ together/forever	Editors usually hate this near-rhyme.
☛ in every way/come what may/ day to day/things you say	Overused and unoriginal.
☛ your birthday's here/ throughout the year	See above.
☛ more and more/ hold in store/	Dated greeting card clichés.

Also: Avoid using the words "grand" and "swell." Although they're easy to rhyme, these adjectives are dated and don't sound conversational.

Your rhyming dictionary is a good source of fresh, new rhyme words. Study it carefully and make a commitment to writing the best constructed verse you possibly can.

Poetic Structure: Additional Techniques

Making sure verse has structure requires more than using perfect meter and wonderful rhyme schemes. Greeting card verse should be poetic. Its structure should help convey the idea behind the card. Several poetic devices are helpful in making greeting card verse memorable.

One technique is to begin each line (or each stanza) with a key phrase to give a greeting card verse poetic impact, as in this quotation from a new baby card:

> *A baby's world* has lullabies
> and cuddly teddy bears . . .
> *A baby's world* has trust and warmth
> and a family that cares . . .
> *A baby's world* has giggly times
> and gentle moments, too . . .
> And a *baby* makes your *world*
> an extra-special dream come true.

Another device is to use an unrhymed refrain to divide the rhyme and meter of a verse, as in the following birthday card for Mom.

> For every jump rope game you played . . .
> For every birthday cake you made . . .
> *Thank you, Mom.*
> For every merry-go-round spin . . .
> For every bedtime tucking-in . . .
> *Thank you, Mom.*
> For every special thing you've done
> To make our home a happy one . . .
> *Thank you, Mom.*

Structure helps your greeting card verse sing. It also helps your verse be logical and organized. But the structure of a verse should not overshadow the me-to-you message. The structure and meaning should work together to create a sendable, original greeting card verse.

But I Hate Writing Verse!

If you find these constrictions to be torturous, or if you can't get the hang of it — some people just don't have an ear for verse — do your editor and yourself a favor and stick to writing prose. *Nothing labels you an amateur faster than a poorly constructed piece of verse.*

Remember that the current demand is greater for humorous and other prose cards, anyway.

WRITING THE NEW GREETING CARD VERSE

If you *do* have the ear and the talent for writing greeting card verse, you may find the perfect market for your work. And even better, you may create messages that touch the hearts of traditional greeting card consumers.

Hallmark editors often ask their writers to come up with "new traditional" card copy. (How's that for an oxymoron?) They are looking for poetic verses written in a conversational style, dealing with contemporary relationships.

I will now walk you through the creative process of writing a new traditional rhymed greeting card.

As you may remember, the three most important rules for writing marketable greeting card verse are *give it structure*, *make it contemporary*, and *make it say something*.

Let's say we want an eight-to-ten-line verse to a stepmother (that makes it contemporary) from a stepdaughter who has finally come to accept and love her (that makes it say something).

We now have two of the essential ingredients for a great greeting card verse. All we have to do is write it:

1. Put the emotions and thoughts you want to express into words. (The poetry comes later!):

You and I have had a difficult time learning to live together. I guess I was jealous of you, and it took me a while to realize that you've always been on my side. But I can see how happy Dad is when he's with you, and I'm grateful to you for making that happen.

2. Find some nice-sounding rhyme words to tie into this verse:
   understand/planned/hand
   side/tried/confide/gratified
   Dad/sad/glad/had/bad
   be/family/me/see

3. Choose a meter within which you'll try to compose this verse. Let's try anapestic (˘ ˘ – / ˘ ˘ –). Here goes:

When you married my dad,	A
I was scared and confused,	B
and you always were patient with me . . .	C
You first earned my trust,	D
then my love and respect,	E
being all a stepmother could be.	C
And I want you to know	F
that I feel very grateful	G
to have you in my family.	C

And that's how you do it. Always start with an idea—preferably an *original* idea. Write the idea out in prose. Find good, strong rhyme words. Choose a structure and meter. Write the verse. Rewrite it. Put it aside. Read it. Rewrite it until you're sure it's the very best you can do.

The workbook in the back of this book includes some exercises in writing traditional verse. Keep practicing, and you may someday find the right words to tell your old English composition teacher "thanks." After all, you're on your way to a fun-filled career as a greeting card writer!

CHAPTER FIVE

"More Than Yesterday, Less Than Tomorrow"
OR

How to Write
Structured Prose

Like rhymed greeting cards, structured, poetic prose cards have been criticized for being contrived, artificial and corny. But people love them, and companies buy writing for them.

This chapter will deal only with structured, poetic prose greeting cards. The rambling, stream-of-consciousness variety of prose proliferating greeting cards of the nineties will be addressed in Chapter Ten, "How to Write Conversational Prose."

The Process of Structured Prose

As when you write greeting card verse, it is important to make each piece of greeting card prose say something. And it is important to give it structure.

I personally feel that structured prose greeting cards are anachronistic. In fact, it helps me to stick a candle in a Chianti bottle and flash back to the sixties and early seventies. Think of Rod McKuen, "Desiderata," *Jonathan Livingston Seagull*, and girls with long hair and bell-bottoms strumming guitars in the park.

Let's go through the process of writing a structured prose greeting card. We know that Editor X at Greeting Card Company Y is buying Christmas ideas right now, and she's looking for romantic prose for "sweetheart."

Here's how you begin:

Make It Say Something

What would a woman want to say to her sweetheart at Christmastime? Jot down some raw material:

I love you. Your love keeps me warm. I feel safe and secure when I'm with you. Christmastime is even more joyful because I have you to share it with.

Use Evocative Language

Some good all-purpose greeting card imagery includes sunrise, sunset, rainbows, dewy rosebuds, landscapes, winterscapes, purple mountains' majesty, candlelight, starry skies, sea gulls and seashores.

Some good *Christmas* imagery includes candlelight, Christmas trees, music, snowfall, firesides, horse-drawn sleighs, families gathering and twinkling lights.

In the Christmas sweetheart card we're writing together, the overwhelming feeling I get is *warmth*. So let's choose the imagery of a fireside to convey the message.

Give It Structure

Like good greeting card verse, structured prose should "sing." In fact, you may want to think of structured prose as being unrhymed poetry. Many poetic inventions are used in creating structured prose greeting cards. Parallel phrases, repetition and alliteration are the most important poetic devices you'll use in creating structured prose cards.

Using the message and imagery we've identified above, let's try using these two writing tricks to create two different structured prose greeting cards for Christmas sweetheart.

Parallel Phrases

When a greeting card message is composed of pairs of similar, parallel phrases, it results in a pleasing, rhythmic effect. This is especially helpful in setting up a metaphor, as I'll do in our Christmas sweetheart example:

> Like firelight fills a home
>> with special warmth,
> your love fills my life
>> with meaning and joy.

One pair of parallel phrases is: "firelight fills a home" and "love fills my life." The other pair of parallel phrases is: "with special warmth" and "with meaning and joy."

Repetition

As with traditional verse writing, repeating a key phrase or idea adds impact and emphasis to structured greeting card prose.

In our Christmas sweetheart example, we'll repeat the key phrase, "Your love keeps me warm." Then, using the imagery of firelight and the romantic feelings we've identified, we'll create another structured prose message.

In our sweet, quiet moments
of caring and sharing,
your love keeps me warm.
With your strength and compassion
and true understanding,
your love keeps me warm.
Like the magical glow
of a yuletide fire burning,
your love keeps me warm.

Alliteration, Internal Rhyme, and Meter

These three poetic devices can also add luster to your structured prose writing. Alliteration, you remember, is the repetition of a beginning consonant sound. We already used alliteration in the first version of our Christmas sweetheart card:

Like *firelight fills* a home
with special warmth,
your *love* fills my *life*
with meaning and joy.

The "f" sound was repeated in line one, and the "l" sound in line three. Really rolls off the tongue, doesn't it?

Let's not overdo alliteration, though, or we might end up with something like:

Like *firelight fills fall*
with wondrous warmth,
your *love loads* my *life*
with *meaning* and *mirth*.

We greeting card writers must be careful not to become parodies of ourselves!

An internal rhyme, obviously, occurs when the rhyme words appear within a line of writing, rather than at the ends of lines. Our second Christmas sweetheart message contains *the* foremost internal rhyme of the greeting card world: *caring* and *sharing*.

We discussed meter in detail in Chapter Four. Be aware that structured prose often has a distinct meter. Our second Christmas sweetheart message employs the anapestic (or "something old, something new") meter. Remember, the "˘" means unstressed, and the "–" means stressed.

> Ĭn oŭr swēet, / qŭiĕt mō / mĕnts
> ŏf cār / ĭng aňd shar / ĭng,
> yŏur lōve / kĕeps mē wārm . . . /

See? It's poetry! If you can master this type of writing, you will be successful not only in creating cards, but in writing words of wisdom for calendars, plaques and posters, too. Chapter Fourteen contains specific writing tips for each of these noncard products.

As with greeting card verse, the big companies have many structured prose cards on file, so your writing must truly be something special to make a sale. But don't be discouraged! If you make your structured prose say something substantive, if you evoke beautiful images loaded with emotion, and if you can give your words an interesting structure, you may find this type of writing enjoyable and profitable.

CHAPTER SIX

"Words of Wisdom"

OR

Writing Inspirational and Religious Cards

With the various spiritual awakenings now happening in society, you can bet the market for religious and inspirational cards is a growth area for many greeting card companies.

There is a simple difference between religious and inspirational cards. Religious cards mention God, Jesus, or some other deity. Inspirational cards, while they may deal with spiritual topics, include no specific mention of a deity.

Many companies (Hallmark, Ambassador, Gibson, American Greetings), include religious and inspirational cards for most seasons and everyday sending situations.

As always, you the writer should be concerned with the general sendability of religious or inspirational cards. As you can guess, the more specific a card's reference is to religion, the less generally sendable it's going to be.

The five messages below are all inspirational or religious greeting card sentiments. They appear in order of their sendability:

May you follow your dreams.	Sendable to anyone.
Wishing you every blessing.	Sendable to believer.
God bless you real good!	Sendable to believer in God.
Smile . . . Jesus Loves You!	Sendable to Christian.
Wishing you blessings as you celebrate another year in our merciful Savior.	Sendable to very specific type of Christian believer.

RELIGIOUS CARDS

There has been a recent change in the writing of religious cards. For lack of a better pair of terms, I'm going to divide religious card writing into two categories: "old religious" and "new religious."

Old Religious

Traditional religious copy would typically be used on a card depicting a Bible and candles, a photo of sunlight streaming through the clouds, a die-cut cross, or other symbol of mainstream Christian religion. (*Note*: Although I refer to this type of greeting card as "old," it is still a staple of the big greeting card companies.) The following is an example of traditional religious birthday copy:

> May God bless you on your birthday
> with His goodness from above —
> May He grant you special happiness
> as He showers you with love.

I'm sure you've read cards like this. They are fairly generic, as religious cards go, and editors' files are full of them. As a freelancer, if you're determined to write and sell traditional religious copy, you must find a way to take a widely sendable idea like this one and make it unique, moving and generally "special." (Let me know if my favorite greeting card word gets on your nerves!)

New Religious

Rather than pursue the rather limited old religious market, it may be more fruitful to address the writing needs of the new religious market. In contrast to old religious cards, new religious designs can range from cute to humorous to boldly graphic. Christian greeting card companies (like Dayspring) provide products for a wide range of Christians, and these companies include messages with very specific references to Christian life.

Here are some examples of the types of messages you might find in a Christian book/card store:

> For birthday:
> Wishing you a joyful walk with the Lord!

> For adult baptism:
> Welcome to God's family!

> For Christmas:
> May the love of the baby Jesus

increase your faith and joy
in the New Year.

For humorous birthday:
*(illustration of rainbows and balloons
pouring down from heaven)*
Hope lots of birthday blessings
are comin' at ya!

The growth of the evangelical Christian movement has freed its followers to express their faith to one another and the world with a directness and intensity not evident in traditional religious cards. And that new expression of Christianity has created a need for fresh and innovative religious writing.

Sincerity is essential when you write religious copy—old or new. It's important to write respectfully and to keep your ideas in good taste.

INSPIRATIONAL CARDS

The market for inspirational writing seems to be growing at an even faster pace than the new religious market. The current spiritual awakening, the end of the "me" decade, and the arrival of "new age" bookstores has expanded the market for inspiring writing.

Once again, I will examine the change in inspirational writing by giving examples of both the "old inspirational" and the "new inspirational" found in greeting card writing.

Old Inspirational

Some famous writers of the old inspirational are Amanda Bradley (Hallmark) and Helen Steiner Rice (Gibson). The following is an example of a traditional inspirational quotation similar to the many beautiful poems written by these venerable grandes dames of greeting cards:

Blessings Are All Around Us
Blessings are all around us . . .
    like the sparkling morning sun
    reflected off the dewdrops,
    making diamonds of each one.

Blessings are all around us . . .
> like the bluebird's cheery song
> awakening our hearts
> and asking them to sing along.

Blessings are all around us
> in nature's vast display . . .
> May we treasure the world's blessings
> as we live and love each day.

As in the example above, many traditional inspirational verses will include images from nature (sunshine, dewdrops, bluebirds — oh, brother!) and a refrain or repeated phrase ("Blessings are all around us . . .") for structure and emphasis. If you can write the kind of poetry your grandma would like to read, traditional inspirational verse may be your niche.

A Note About Quotations

"Words of wisdom" such as those in the preceding example are called "quotations" or "quotes." They differ from other greeting card writing in that the thought contains no me-to-you message.

Quotations can be as simple as "Sharing Is Caring" or as long and flowery as "What Is a Mother?"

Freelance opportunities exist for selling quotations with complementary me-to-you messages. The various religious card publishers rely heavily on this format in their greeting card lines.

You can also find a literary or biblical quotation and then write a me-to-you message referring to the quotation.

For example, I've decided to write a religious wedding card to go with the following biblical verse:

> So faith, hope, and love abide,
> these three; but the greatest of these is love.
> 1 Corinthians 13:13

The key words in the following verse are *faith*, *hope* and *love*. I might try creating a nice prose wish that uses three complementary me-to-you messages:

> May the promise of this day
> fill your hearts with faith . . .
> May the beauty of this day
> fill your lives with hope . . .
> May the Lord bless and keep you
> and fill all your days with love.

As you can see, matching a quotation with a me-to-you message can have a terrific emotional impact.

New Inspirational

The nineties look to be a very spiritual decade for many people. People are interested in the cosmic relationship between themselves and God, their fellow people, and the universe.

Writing for this new type of spirituality might include the following types of greeting card messages:

Affirmations

These are statements of personal dreams, abilities and empowerment:

> I am calm and confident,
> and with each breath,
> I take in the wonder of the universe.

The idea behind affirmations is that people read and reread positive messages to reprogram their brains to function more positively.

Messages of Love and Friendship

Spiritual people tend to nurture their connection to other humans. Cards could address the spiritual side of friendship, love and family:

> I've only just met you,
> yet I feel we've been together
> since the beginning of time.

Messages of Support

For people in recovery from addiction or depression, the support of friends is very important. Hazelden, an addiction treatment center in

Minnesota, already offers several small lines of greeting cards and related products in its direct mail catalog.

An example of a supportive greeting card message might be:

Congratulations
on a whole year of sobriety . . .
one day at a time!

Both religious and inspirational cards are important parts of the social expression industry. To a writer, selling a pearl of wisdom or some words of encouragement can feel very rewarding. After all, your writing could make a big difference in someone's day!

CHAPTER SEVEN

"Beyond Duckies and Bunnies"
OR

How to Write Great Juvenile Cards

The opportunity for freelancers in juvenile cards is not as great as in other areas. However, I couldn't omit this chapter on writing juvenile cards: I spent two years at Hallmark planning the juvenile line, and "juvies" are my favorite products to work with!

The best way to get ideas for juvenile cards is to spend some time with kids. If you do not have any live-in children, consider visiting a playground, a video arcade, a G-rated movie, an amusement park, a circus or a soccer field. If you do not have the time or stomach for these rather intense voyages into juvenile-land, watch Saturday morning TV, read kids' magazines, visit the children's section of your public library, or get a good book on child development.

Whichever method of "research" you use, take notes. What feelings do children have? What words do they use? What might the adults in the children's lives need to communicate to them? What specific activities do kids of certain ages enjoy? What juvenile properties (licensed characters) are currently popular? Why do you think these have such great appeal among children? I believe that asking these kinds of questions makes the difference between writing "just average" juvenile cards and creating big winners.

BIRTHDAY AND SEASONAL JUVENILE CARDS

Juvenile cards have changed dramatically since the early eighties. Where once they depicted mostly duckies and chickies, sweet little girls bringing gifts, and "little sluggers" holding baseball bats, the subject matter now reflects the interests of children today. Dinosaurs, rocket ships, girls playing soccer, guitars, ninja turtles, and roller coasters are likely subject matter for juvenile cards in the nineties.

For the writing to keep up with these changes in subject matter, we writers needed to move beyond the "standard" four-line verse:

> This cute little [fuzzy animal]
>> is coming your way
> To wish you a happy
>> [Whatever] Day!

Here are some suggestions for bringing your juvenile card writing into the nineties.

Talk About Feelings

How must a child feel on his or her birthday? What feelings are associated with growing up? What mixed feelings do parents have as their children grow up? What does a parent want to say at Christmas to a toddler? To a ten-year-old? Making your messages honest and insightful is the surest way to grab some mom's or auntie's (*or editor's*) heartstrings.

Here's an example of a poignant juvenile card:

> *To My Daughter With Love*
> I used to think you were one of the
> sweetest little girls in the world . . .
> now I think you're one of the sweetest *big* girls!

Warm compliments are a must in *all* juvenile captions. After all, these are very special kids you're dealing with!

Be Silly

Use fanciful ideas, messages and images to suggest wild and funny illustrations. Remember the things you giggled about when you were a child?

Try to use those memories to create a card that captures everyone's shared childhood experiences.

For example:

> On your birthday,
> hope you laugh so hard
> that milk comes out your nose!

(Kids love humor.)

Have Fun With Words

Obscure rhymes and outrageous alliteration are *made* for juvenile cards. One approach that's especially fun is to create a fictitious character to set up in a birthday situation with a fun poem:

> Andrea the Android
>> brought a big bionic cake
> With neat robotic Candle-oids
>> for the wishes that you'll make!
> Andrea is programmed
>> to perform a song for you—
> "Happy Birthday to a Humanoid
>> who's sweet and special, too!"

This juvenile verse does the unexpected. It makes a robot *female*. It uses funny words like candle-oid and humanoid. And it alliterates the words Andrea and Android.

Whether your wordplay is a painful knock-knock joke or a corny riddle, remember: These are kids you're dealing with; it's all *new* to them!

Remember Who Buys the Card

Almost all juvenile cards are purchased by grown-ups. So create a product that reflects what *you* think a *grown-up* thinks a *child* thinks is appealing.

For example, you may think that a graffiti-covered wall is good subject matter for a teen card. But the adult who purchases the card probably won't find vandalism very humorous.

Write Like a Child Talks

Juvenile birthday and seasonal cards are of two basic types: adult-to-child and child-to-adult. In the child-to-adult captions, such as "Grandma from child," "Mommy from child," "Daddy from child," etc., childlike language is very important.

My children and I play a game at bedtime in which we try to create metaphors for how much we love each other. I might start by saying, "I love you as much as five elephants." And my six-year-old might say, "I love you as much as the whole ocean." The most beautiful poem to come out of this bedtime ritual was my son Joey's:

I love you as big
as a bird flies up to the sky.

One technique to get into your "child" state is to write with a crayon, using your nondominant hand (use your left if you're right-handed, and vice versa). Then ask yourself, "What would I have liked to tell my daddy on his birthday? Or my grandma on Mother's Day?"

These kinds of messages—raw emotion expressed in childlike imagery—make for great juvenile greeting cards.

Don't Be Sexist

Little girls play sports, too. Little boys can have teddy bears. Avoid implying that little girls are passive wimps and that little boys are *always* rough-and-tumble rascals. (And you thought greeting card writing wasn't political!)

Juvenile Activity Cards

A small percentage of juvenile cards is composed of "activity cards"—mazes, secret messages, crossword puzzles, games, put-together puppets, etc. These generally are written in-house to facilitate the collaboration of artist and writer.

If you are determined to write juvenile activity cards, make sure these cards are more than a gimmick. Don't lose the warmth of the message to the contrivance of the card.

NON-OCCASION JUVENILE CARDS

Until recently, the market for juvenile greeting cards was limited to birthday and seasonal cards. With its introduction of the "To Kids With Love" line, however, Hallmark expanded juvenile card sending situations to include "anyday" feelings such as "I'm sorry," "I'm proud of you," and "I wish we could be together."

This new line reflects in part the changing dynamic of the American family. Card companies (and card writers) can no longer assume that the parent who is purchasing a juvenile card is the parent who lives with the recipient child. Also, the importance of other significant adults (day-care providers and stepparents, for example) in a child's life create a need for new types of communication and sharing.

Now that Hallmark has plunged into the non-occasion juvenile market, we can assume that the bandwagon effect will have other companies following suit. This may be a growing market for freelance greeting card writing. By using the juvenile writing tips in this chapter and the suggestions in Chapter Ten, "How to Write Conversational Prose," you can write successfully for this market.

CHAPTER EIGHT

"I Wuv You Bunches!"
OR

Writing Cute and Whimsical Cards

hen a greeting card makes you smile and say "Awwwww," the card is probably in the "cute" category. (This big-selling category can also be referred to as "informals," "whimsicals," or even "soft humor.") You know the type of card—adorable little girls with big eyes and baskets of flowers, koala bears hanging upside down on trees, baby bluebirds chirping in a frilly curtained window. Cute or informal cards are among the best-selling greeting cards. And when a company has an opportunity to sell a lot of cards, we writers have an opportunity to sell a lot of ideas.

Cute cards are included in all seasons and in most everyday captions (with the possible exception of "sympathy"). They can be written in either prose or verse, and most cute cards are no longer than four lines.

THE MARRIAGE OF WORDS AND PICTURES

It is important to think visually when you write cute copy, because the tie-in of design and words is what makes a cute concept work. If you cannot draw, learn to describe your visual ideas in words. ("Thinking Visually" in the Workbook section gives you some practice in creating these total concepts.)

Let's look at two ways to write cute cards: (1) starting with the words, and (2) starting with the pictures. Both are valid methods.

Starting With the Words

A very simple message, such as "thinking of you with love," can evolve into a strong total idea when a writer suggests a unique visual image to go with it. Here are some whimsical or cute design suggestions for the copy, "thinking of you with love":

- ☛ A clown whose juggling balls form a heart pattern in the air.

- ☛ An angel resting comfortably and contentedly on a fluffy heart-shaped cloud.

- ☛ An anthropomorphic mouse baking heart-shaped cookies.

- ☛ A little girl drawing a chalk heart on the sidewalk.

☛ A little girl tracing a heart on a frosty window.

☛ A little girl lying on her back watching a heart-shaped
flock of geese fly over.

(Okay, we're getting a little bizarre here. But these six examples came right off the top of my head.)

In each example, the idea of "thinking of you with love" is enhanced by a design that makes you go, "Awwwww!"

Starting With the Pictures

Sometimes a knock-out design concept will come to you first. Then you'll write some exceptional copy to reinforce the design.

For example, right now I'm looking out my window, and my golden retriever and our neighbor's cockapoo are standing nose-to-nose through the back fence. They're both jumping around and wagging their tails like crazy. (Kind of makes you go, "Awwwww," doesn't it?)

Let's see, what kinds of cute messages might work with a design of a golden retriever and a cockapoo playing nosies through the fence?

It could be a message about how they like each other in spite of their differences:

The way that you're you
and the way that I'm me
Make every day
as fun as can be!

Or about the frustration of being separated:

Sure would be nice
if we could get together sometime!

Or I could use some "dog" or "fence" words to create a punned message:

"How are things on your side of the fence?"
or
"How's tricks?"

Of these examples, the first card I wrote is probably the most original and, therefore, the most marketable one.

The creative processes and tricks described in chapter two are extremely helpful in creating cute concepts. With practice, a writer's mind can go quickly back and forth between *visual images* and *verbal ideas*.

EXAMPLE: Let's say you're writing cards for a client who has a Christmas/cute project. Once again, I will transcribe what a writer's brain might do when confronted with this challenge:

What are some good Christmas animals? Penguins, polar bears, reindeer, huskies, timberwolves. How about some Christmas words? Season's greetings. Holiday greetings. Let's try a polar bear saying, "Holiday Grrrrreetings!" What if Santa drove a dog sled instead of his sleigh? What's a good dogsled word? Mush! "Merry Christmas with love . . . and all that mush!" Which animals might look cute caroling? Which animals would look cute building a snow sculpture? Mice. What if you had cats building a snow cat and mice building a snow mouse? It could say, "Peace on Earth."

Cute copy is a *must* for a freelance card writer's bag of creative tricks. The cute market cuts across the juvenile, feminine, teen and senior citizen card-buying public; most companies always have room for a new and innovative treatment of this best-selling type of card.

CHAPTER NINE

"I Just Flew In From Hallmark, and Boy Are My Arms Tired!"

OR

How to Write Traditional Humor

In recent years, traditional greeting card humor has taken a back seat to the wacky variety practiced by creative geniuses such as Sandra Boynton, Barbara and Jim Dale, Gary Larson and Nicole Hollander. But it's important to know how to write "good old, good old" humorous cards, because the big companies still offer traditional humor in their lines. And, you never know: The pendulum may swing back toward puns, knock-knocks and hillbilly jokes faster than you can say "happy birthday, young 'un."

(Incidentally, many of the successful alternative humor writers actually employ formulas and techniques that have been around since the dawn of greetingdom. But don't tell them I told you.)

Let's take a look at traditional humor in three chunks: (1) humorous/illustrated, (2) studio/contemporary and (3) licensed properties.

HUMOROUS/ILLUSTRATED

Have you ever been shopping for a nice birthday card for your mother and noticed — right next to the bluebirds, flowers and butterflies — the goofy cards with animated grapes, silly-looking dogs and cats, and photos of dressed-up monkeys? These are humorous/illustrated cards. The writing for this market is broad, punny and complimentary — *never* esoteric, subtle or snide. Humorous/illustrated cards are included in most major everyday and season captions.

It's a good idea when writing humorous/illustrated cards to start with a basic unifying concept or idea. This is important, because you are trying to communicate something very abstract — feelings — in very simple, concrete pictures and words.

Humorous/illustrated cards can be written in either verse or prose. We'll write one verse and one prose card, and then you'll get some more practice in the Workbook section.

Humorous/Illustrated Verse

I personally believe that writing humorous verse is a lost art. Not many freelancers can do it, so if you're good, you could make some money at it.

At Hallmark, writers call the humorous cards that feature a long verse suggesting a series of illustrations "rebus" cards. Suggesting illustrations to complement your copy helps improve your chances of selling rebus cards. (Other companies may use different terminology. When in doubt, ask your editor for examples.) Rebus cards can use either description or metaphor or simile to communicate their messages.

Description

Descriptive rebuses detail the wonderful traits and behavior of the recipient. These cards can describe a group of people:

COPY	DESIGN
Babies are wigglers	Baby in jumping swing
and gurglers and gigglers . . .	Babies tickling each other
They're kissers and huggers and on camera muggers!	Baby giving sloppy kiss Baby peeking upside-down between legs

Or they can describe one very specific recipient:

For all the times you'd chauffeur me,	Mom in taxi
and all the jeans you'd sew for me,	Mom patching tattered jeans
Thank you, Mom.	

Metaphor or Simile

Metaphor or simile rebuses make a comparison of the recipient to some humorous (and fun-to-illustrate) thing. Sometimes this metaphor or simile is spelled out in the verse:

COPY	DESIGN
Daughters are like a magazine—	(Each design looks like a magazine cover)
Some are full of news,	Daughter of the Year!
Some upset their parents with their controversial views	Daughter burning bra

If the metaphor is not spelled out in the verse, it is illustrated in the design and alluded to in the verse; for example, the following copy is for a design of movie posters showing different types of movies:

COPY	DESIGN
Some husbands are disasters, with all their foolish gaffes—	Movie poster: "The Towering Klutz!"
Some are just plain silly, they'll do anything for laughs!	Movie poster: "The Thomas *Clown* Affair"

How do you write one of these cards? First of all, know who your audience is. As you may have already gathered from the examples above, humorous/illustrated purchasers are among the most traditional members of the greeting card public.

The market also tends to be more masculine than other social expression markets. Think Benny Hill, Fozzie Bear, Henny Youngman . . . you get the idea.

Let's say that I have received a letter from an editor asking for contributions to a humorous/illustrated "masculine birthday" project. The company is looking for new verse treatments of this very traditional form of writing.

Once again, I try to transcribe my thoughts as I start creating. Let's start with the simile, "Dads are like pizzas." (Bear with me here.) I think this is a good unifying concept. No, wait. Not dads. Brothers. Brothers are like pizzas. Brothers and pizzas go together better. I can see some very funny illustrations of animated pizzas. This is gonna be good. (I find this positive self-talk to be very helpful, since I do most of my humor writing from the relative vacuum of my home office.)

Okay. Brothers are like pizzas. Brothers are like pizzas. Where do I go from here?

First, I make a humorous/illustrated concept chart (see page 87).

Now I'm rolling. It's time to pick out a meter in which to write this little gem. I choose a simple iambic ("The queen of hearts, she made some tarts") meter.

HUMOROUS/ILLUSTRATED CONCEPT:
"Brothers are like pizzas"

IMAGES:	WORDS:
Pepperoni	Spicy, all-time favorite.
Supreme combo	I don't want to lay it on too thick, but, Brother, you're SUPREME!
Cheese	Some brothers think they're the "big cheese."
Onion	Some brothers make you cry.
Dough	Some brothers have a lot of dough.
Crust	Some brothers are crusty.
Vegetarian	Some brothers "veg out" all the time.

Sŏme brŏth / eřs hāve / ă lōt / ŏf crūst, /
sŏme hāve / ă lōt / ŏf doūgh! /

What rhymes with *dough*? Go. Flow. So. Know!

Sŏme brŏth / eřs aře / "bĭg chēes / eš" —
thĕy're aī / wăys iñ / the knōw! /

Next I have to start thinking about how to wrap this up with a nice compliment for Brother. The "combo supreme" idea is a good one. But what rhymes with *supreme*? Now I look in my rhyming dictionary, and the word *scream* jumps out at me.

Sŏme brŏth / eřs līke / tŏ māke / yŏu crȳ, /
sŏme ōth / eřs māke / yŏu scrēam — /
Bŭt yoū're / the pēr / fĕct cōm / bŏ— /
ă brŏth / ĕr who's / SŬPRĒME! /

We did it! Let's see how it looks:

> Some brothers have a lot of crust,
>   some have a lot of dough,
> Some brothers are "big cheeses" —
>   they're always in the know!
> Some brothers like to make you cry,
>   some like to make you scream —
> But you're the "perfect combo,"
>   a brother who's SUPREME!

See? It just *begs* to be illustrated!

When I submit this rebus card, my submission (with design suggestions) might look like this:

> (illustration of animated pizza crust)
> Some brothers have a lot of crust,
>   some have a lot of dough,
>
> (illustration of animated cheese)
> Some brothers are "big cheeses" —
>   they're always in the know!
>
> (illustration of animated onions)
> Some brothers like to make you cry,
>
> (illustration of "HOT HOT HOT" peppers)
>   some like to make you scream —
> But you're the "perfect combo,"
>   a brother who's SUPREME!

By using the humorous/illustrated concept chart, you can create many different verses. Just decide on the sending situation (brother birthday or husband anniversary, for example), find a set of images that strikes you as funny, and go for it.

Making these images current or trendy is one way of bringing rebus verse into the nineties. Allude to top TV shows, fashion trends and current events. Be careful, though, of flash-in-the-pan fads that may fade quickly from the memory and heart of greeting card consumers.

Humorous/Illustrated Prose

Writing humorous/illustrated prose is similar to writing humorous/ illustrated verse. You need some good, visual, literal concepts to work with. The difference is that now you're basically writing one-liners, so you don't have to wring every last joke out of each concept.

Think knock-knocks, puns (even real groaners), riddles, wordplay and "mechanics" (no, not the kind in coveralls). Mechanics are the gimmicky folds used for surprise effect in some humorous cards. These devices enable characters to pop up out of the top of a card, reach out for a hug, or pucker up for a kiss.

Again, let's create a typical freelance situation. We are working on a humorous/illustrated project for Valentine's Day. The editor wants puns, mechanicals and "general gags."

Puns

Puns and wordplay are right at home on humorous/illustrated cards. One way to get started is to make an idea starter sheet of words and feelings appropriate to the project you're working on—in this case, Valentine's Day:

Hugs	Be Mine
Kisses	Valentine
Sweetheart	Cupid

Then work your way down the list trying to make sendable puns from the words:

Hugs and Kisses. Hogs and Quiches? No. It's been done. Hucks and Kitchens? This isn't going well. How about a pun on the word "sex"? Sects. Sax. Sacks. Be mine? Bee mind? Bee mime? *A definite maybe!*

(OUTSIDE): (illustration of a bee in white face with
black-and-white costume):
(INSIDE): Honeybee Mime!

Mechanical Cards

To write mechanical cards, make an idea starter sheet listing the types of folds and gimmicks that might work for this writing effort:

☛ Pop-ups

☛ Kissy lips

☛ Huggy arms

☛ Character falling down swooning

Then start the creative gears grinding:

What body part could pop up from inside the card? No! Not *that* body part. How about Cupid shooting a pop-up arrow into the air? What could the card say? What do *my* kids say when *they're* shooting each other? "You got me!" Now we're making progress!

> (OUTSIDE): (design of cupid shooting arrow at
> character):
> Sweetheart, YOU GOT ME . . .
> (INSIDE): (three-dimensional character has fallen down
> swooning):
> . . . right where you want me!
> Happy Valentine's Day With Love

The card above is an example of how inspiration can come from many directions at once. I combined a technical greeting card *format* with Valentine *imagery* and my day-to-day *experience*, and a brand-new idea was created. You can do this, too. Just open your eyes, ears and mind to everything that's out there. (Chapter Fourteen describes this process in detail.)

General Gags

Writing humorous/illustrated general gags is much easier once you learn to work with various humorous/illustrated formulas and devices.

Here's how you might write some Valentines using several familiar formulas:

Negative/Positive Switch

The cover of the card, an insult, is turned into a compliment on the inside:

> (OUTSIDE): You are a very sick person . . .
> (INSIDE): . . . just what I'm looking for in a Valentine!

The outside "slam" is saved by the positive message inside.

Return to the Literal

Think of a familiar cliché and how it might be illustrated *literally*:

(OUTSIDE): (illustration of refrigerator shelf with
jalapeños, salsa, picante sauce, etc.):
(INSIDE): Happy Valentine's Day, Hot Stuff!

Surprise Inside

The cover is a stock opening greeting card line, but inside is an unpredictable message:

(OUTSIDE): (stock opening line):
Valentine, you've made me
what I am today . . .
(INSIDE): (panting horse illustration):
. . . hot to trot!

Before you turn up your nose at writing this and other types of formulaic humor, remember that many consumers feel more comfortable in familiar humorous territory. That's why an audience can enjoy the work of one particular comedian show after show after show. People watch "The Honeymooners" reruns repeatedly. Why? They like Jackie Gleason's brand of humor.

The same is true of your greeting card audience. If you write humorous/illustrated cards, remember that a sizable share of the card-buying public goes to *that* particular rack looking for *that* particular type of humor. And although you work within the parameters of certain age-old formulas, this type of writing is great mental exercise. After all, you're taking something very traditional and trying to make it sound innovative and fresh.

STUDIO/CONTEMPORARY

These have traditionally been the long, skinny, funny cards, although this physical format appears to be on the way out. Studio humor has a harder edge than humorous/illustrated, probably because the purchasers are younger.

The studio/contemporary cards of yesteryear often were illustrated with a funny little nebbish extending his forefinger. Greeting card artists call these guys "neuters," because the characters were intended to represent "everyperson" in the greeting card buying world; that is, they could be sent to either men or women.

While the captions for humorous/illustrated cards include almost *all* everyday and season sending situations, studio/contemporary captions are more limited. Typically, companies include the following captions in their everyday studio/contemporary lines:

BIRTHDAY	FRIENDSHIP
General wish	Love/suggestive
Compliment	Thinking of you
Age slam	Close relationship
Age compliment	Keep in touch
To man	Sorry I haven't written
To woman	Timely or topical
Celebrate	
Belated	
From both	
From all	
Twenty-first	
Fortieth	
Relative	

CHEER	MISCELLANEOUS
Get well	Congratulations
Hospital	Retirement
Operation	Goodbye
From all	Goodbye from all
Accident	Baby congratulations
	New home

ANNIVERSARY _____

General (not wedding)

Wedding

Our wedding

The following are the major seasons for studio/contemporary cards:

New Year's	Graduation
Valentine's Day	Father's Day
St. Patrick's Day	Halloween
Easter	Thanksgiving
April Fool's Day	Christmas
Mother's Day	

Within these seasons, stick to the most generally sendable studio/contemporary captions. Gags about the specific events and traditions of the season work best.

Studio/Contemporary Formulas

Let's walk through the major formulas for studio/contemporary cards. Even if you *hate* this kind of writing, learn to do it! To a certain extent, humor is humor, and mastering the formulas will help you understand why things will (or won't) work.

In the humorous/illustrated section of this chapter, we learned three humor formulas: (1) the negative/positive switch, (2) the return to the literal, and (3) the surprise inside. These formulas also work in studio/contemporary, although the humor within the formulas should be somewhat more caustic, hip and/or suggestive.

For example, let's look at the negative/positive switch we wrote for humorous/illustrated:

(OUTSIDE): (slam): You are a very sick person . . .
(INSIDE): (saved by positive message):
. . . just what I'm looking for in a Valentine!

To make this a studio/contemporary card, we might change the cover to the more blatant "You're an insatiable sex maniac . . ."

Similarly, let's revise the surprise inside Valentine we wrote:

> (OUTSIDE): (stock opening line):
> Valentine, you've made me
> what I am today . . .
> (INSIDE): (panting horse):
> . . . hot to trot!

For the studio/contemporary market, we can make the punch line or payoff more explicit:

> (OUTSIDE): (stock opening line):
> Valentine, you've made me
> what I am today . . .
> (INSIDE): . . . a trembling mass of quivering flesh!

This example also points out another difference between studio/contemporary and humorous/illustrated cards. There is, generally speaking, no illustration inside a studio/contemporary card—so your words must carry the idea.

Here are some more studio/contemporary formulas. Different card writers may call these by different names, but the examples and definitions should illustrate how they work:

Exaggeration

The message *overstates* the wish or feeling the sender is trying to communicate.

> (OUTSIDE): You're the cat's pajamas—
> (INSIDE): As a matter of fact,
> you're well on your way to becoming his
> bathrobe!

Understatement

The message *understates* the wish or feeling the sender is trying to communicate.

(OUTSIDE): I think about you every now and then . . .

(INSIDE): . . . and also every "whenever" in between!

Reverse

This approach switches around the normal relationship between the images in a cliché.

(OUTSIDE): (illustration of a silly ant):
Every time I think of how much
I miss you . . .

(INSIDE): . . . I get *people* in my pants!

Repetition

A phrase from the cover of the card is repeated inside (with a punch line added), as in this "card gag":

(OUTSIDE): Don't think of this as just another birthday
card . . .

(INSIDE): . . . think of it as just another birthday present!

Parody

This card plays off a familiar phrase, song, movie or book, as shown in the following age slam:

(OUTSIDE): (illustration of aging rockers):
We were born to run . . .

(INSIDE): . . . of course, that was many years ago!

I encourage you to use these formulas to help you start writing studio/contemporary cards. But don't let them limit you! Study the card racks of your potential clients to find *new* formulas or approaches that seem to work for them. And don't be afraid to try some wacky, off-the-wall approaches from time to time. These will be discussed in greater detail in Chapter Eleven, "Writing the 'New Humor' Cards and Promotions," but remember that most editors are eager to stretch the boundaries of their respective card lines — even traditional lines like humorous/illustrated and studio/contemporary.

The writing tricks in Chapter Two also will help you create funny and marketable cards for this market.

LICENSED PROPERTIES

In greeting cards, as in much of popular culture, products featuring licensed properties are in great demand. Whether they're TV characters, rock stars or animated creatures, consumers like to identify with familiar faces.

Don't submit writing for licensed properties unless you are sure your client buys freelance writing for this product category. If an editor's needs list includes writing for one of these properties, it is worthwhile to research all the characters within that property to learn their personalities and functions. Using the humorous/illustrated and studio/contemporary formulas and techniques becomes a new challenge with the added constriction of characters' personality differences.

Sometimes a freelance writer or illustrator can sell a company an entire group of cards (or a "promotion") featuring an original character of his or her own creation. If you are thinking of pursuing this challenge, be sure to get your ideas trademarked or copyrighted to protect your legal ownership of the work. Writing greeting card promotions is also addressed in Chapter Eleven.

As I stated, the types of writing described in this chapter are not an area of growth for most companies. Still, I'm sure you'll find that your traditional humor writing skills will enhance your versatility and your marketability as a freelance social expression writer.

Alternative
Greeting
Cards

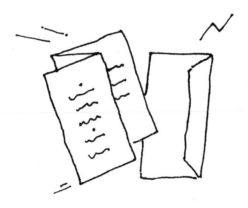

CHAPTER TEN

"Letter Writing for Hire"

OR

How to Write Conversational Prose

As mentioned in Chapter One, an explosion hit the social expression industry in the early eighties. While giant companies such as Hallmark, Ambassador and American Greetings built their empires on *knowing* the rules of greeting cards, the smaller companies—such as Recycled Paper, Maine Line and Paper Moon—built their success on *breaking* the rules.

In the mid-eighties, these innovative young companies became a serious threat to the larger companies' market shares. It appeared that consumer demand had shifted from cards with elaborate artwork and sentimental, poetic-sounding copy, to simpler designs, blunt-edged humor, and honest communication.

As the giants lost business to these smaller companies, retailers pressured the larger companies to provide "alternative" products that would reflect the change in the card-buying public's tastes. Hallmark responded with Shoebox Greetings, American Greetings with its 78th Street line, and soon all the big companies were following suit. Before long, *everybody* was doing alternative cards. This brings us to the irony of the nineties: If everyone's doing "alternative" cards, they're not really alternative anymore!

Nevertheless, this new style of writing and designing appears to be the major growth area for greeting cards. In the following chapters we'll learn to write both serious and humorous cards for the alternative market. We'll take a look at "non-occasion" cards, the newest cards on the block, and we'll speculate on what's coming next in the world of social expression.

I deliberately saved the alternative cards for last. Although these products are less bound by the conventions of traditional card writing, you will be a better and more knowledgeable writer of alternative cards if you acquire the basic, tried-and-true skills of the trade.

WHAT IS CONVERSATIONAL PROSE?

While serious prose on greeting cards once was stiff, formal and structured, the "new" greeting cards express ideas in a direct, chatty, casual, and even stream-of-consciousness style. This kind of writing is called "conversational prose."

Conversational prose cards usually are illustrated with abstract watercolor designs. They often have provocative titles, such as "I'm Worried About You" or "You Changed My Life." You will recognize these cards by their *pastel* watercolor designs, *personal* titles (such as "I Need More Time for Myself," "Let's Be More Than Just Friends," or "You're Getting On My Nerves") followed by *profuse* hand-lettered copy. Aha! I have accidentally hit on the "Three P's" of conversational prose: pastel, personal and profuse.

This writing skill is closely related to writing dialogue for a movie, novel or play. To be any good, it has to sound exactly the way people talk. More specifically, it has to sound exactly the way people talk when they try to say something emotional or difficult.

The following are some specific rules for writing conversational prose:

Write a Killer Opening Line

The beginning of the message should give the consumer (and the recipient) a fairly good idea of what's being communicated. There's plenty of room in these cards for hemming and hawing around, but don't do it in the first line.

Write the Way People Talk

I already said this, but it's important, so I'm telling you again. Avoid all traditional "greeting cardisms."

Here's a good exercise for developing a good ear for dialogue. Next time you're out for breakfast or lunch, ask for a booth. From the moment you sit down, transcribe the conversation that's going on in the booth behind you.

People talk differently from the way they write. If you can capture the sincerity and spontaneity of a warm heart-to-heart talk, you will excel at this type of writing.

Balance the Specific With the General

You want your card to get the reaction, "This is *exactly* what I want to say to so-and-so!" If you are too specific, the reaction might be, "Who would ever send a weird card like *this*?" If you are too general, people may think, "Who would ever send a boring card like *this*?"

One way to guarantee that your card is unique is to think of two specific people, a sender and a recipient, for whom you create a message. Give them personalities, issues, histories, and even names if you want. Then think of the specific feelings those people might have for each other, and write them in *the sender's* own words.

Grope for Words

If there's one thought that seems to proliferate on conversational prose cards, it's the old "words cannot express" concept. After all, if the purchaser were eloquent and communicative, there would be no need for a person in the middle to put ink on paper.

Cards for many different sending situations can and do touch on the difficulty of communicating our feelings to one another. Some key phrases to convey this feeling are: "This isn't easy to say, but . . ." "How can I ever tell you how much you mean?" "I may not always say this in so many words . . ." "We're not the type to talk about our feelings . . ." and "We haven't had much time for talking lately."

Don't Just "Type"

Frankly, some conversational prose cards strike me as being just plain "typing," without structure, purpose or point. You know the kind I mean:

> You're a wonderful and special person,
>> and just knowing you're around
> can make me feel a whole lot better
>> about the world.
> So on your birthday
>> I hope you realize what an important
> part of my life you've always been.

Nice thoughts, yes. A good greeting card, no. Somewhere amidst all the "hope you realizes" and "just knowing you're arounds," a writer needs to inject some poetry. Not contrived, sappy pap, but some kind of special structure or imagery to make the prose click with consumers. (We'll work on this when we create a conversational prose card together.)

Be aware that these cards are everywhere in the big companies' lines. You will find conversational prose even in the most traditional captions, both everyday and seasonal. So don't limit your efforts to writing for the big promotion of watercolor cards at the front of the store.

If your client's greeting card line has *few* conversational prose cards, the writing will need to be more general and less experimental. Be creative and logical in the marketing, as well as the writing, of your cards.

WRITING CONVERSATIONAL PROSE

Now let's write a card. As I did in the traditional chapters, I will take you through the mental process of writing conversational prose. This time, I'll assume that I have a project assignment from an editor.

Here's the type of request I might receive:

"We are building a line of conversational prose cards for people who are in changing relationships. I need writing for those whose love is fading, or growing, or stagnating. I need writing for friends who've drifted apart, or rediscovered each other, or who've had an argument. In short, I need copy for people in all stages of all kinds of relationships.

"I'm especially interested in long conversational copy with a unique twist or unusual point of view. When you write, please think of real people with names and faces, and write especially for them."

Because this is a project and not a specific assignment, I am free to choose the situations for which I will write. While this freedom is a luxury, it also gives a writer the added burden of choosing a unique, yet plausible, sending situation.

Here are the steps I might go through when working on a conversational prose project:

Choose a Sending Situation

I visit the editor's card rack and find that there is a glut of cards dealing with a couple's *need* to address problems, the *need* to communicate more, the *need* to be together. . . . Need, schmeed. I'm going to write a card for couples who are *too* enmeshed, who talk *too* much about their problems, who are getting a little sick of each other's company.

Key Phrases

Jot down some key phrases and feelings to capture the relationship of this couple: "I need some time to myself." "You're smothering me." "It seems we never see our friends anymore." "We're in our own little world, and that used to be fine, but we need to get out more." "We talk about our relationship so much that some of the relaxed spontaneity is gone."

The Opening Sentence

Remember, this needs to capture the essence of what you're about to say. Also, when the message is about a problem or concern (as ours is), it's best to start out with an affirmation of the sender's affection, friendship or concern.

Here goes:

> I really like being with you,
> but I think we're spending too much time
> in our own little world.

It states the premise, it starts out upbeat, *and* it has a metaphor ("our own little world").

Order Your Ideas

Construct a logical progression of the ideas you want to communicate:

- ☛ I like being with you.
- ☛ Too much time in our own little world.
- ☛ I miss our friends.
- ☛ I miss my friends, too.
- ☛ And I miss having time to myself.
- ☛ It takes two *complete* people to make a strong relationship.
- ☛ We're spending all our energy on each other.

☛ I want us to be the best we can be — when we're
together and when we're apart.

Write the Card

We already have our opening. All we have to do is polish the feelings
and phrases we've listed above:

> I really like being with you,
>> but I think we're spending too much time
>> in our own little world.
>
> I miss our friends. I miss my friends, too.
> And I miss having time to myself.
> It takes two complete people
>> to make a good relationship,
>> and when we spend so much energy
>> on being a couple,
>> it's hard to grow as individuals.
>
> I want us to be happy and fulfilled
>> together *and* apart.
>
> So let's open up our world
>> just a little
>> and become the best we both can be.

As you can see, the key phrases and feelings evolved quite a bit
between steps four and five (the list of ideas and the finished card). It
took some trial and error, but we now have a greeting card. A good one,
too, I think. It says something new. It's honest and direct. Yet it sounds
softly poetic when it refers to "our little world."

For this type of writing, advice columns in newspapers or magazines
are a good source of material. TV too, can provide interesting personas
to work with. (What might June Cleaver have said to Ward when he was
too hard on "The Beave"?)

The possibilities for writing conversational prose cards are as infinite
as the possibilities of feelings in human relationships. Whether or not
it's your favorite type of writing (and it's *not* mine!), conversational prose
can even be helpful in working through personal conflicts.

And, of course, if you succeed, this fast-growing market could make
you lots of money, too!

CHAPTER ELEVEN

"The Wild, the Weird, and the Wacko"

OR

Writing the "New Humor" Cards and Promotions

Like serious prose, humor writing changed dramatically in the eighties. The "new humor" cards looked and sounded simple, honest, casual and sassy, not at all like the formulaic slams and rebus verse.

THE FEMINIZATION OF HUMOR

While we greeting card professionals have always known that our consumers are primarily women, up until the early eighties, the writing and illustration of humorous greeting cards was noticeably masculine. And for good reason. Almost all the people writing and drawing humor were *men*.

But when greeting card humorists such as Sandra Boynton, Cathy Guisewite and Nicole Hollander achieved phenomenal success with acutely female subject matter such as dieting, men-as-jerks, fashion, beauty and exercise, even the big companies were forced to open their locker rooms to the feminine point of view.

Many of the characteristics of the new humor reflect this feminization of the greeting card industry. I will look at several characteristics of the new humor. Bear in mind that these categories are not mutually exclusive, and, in fact, some of the best cards may combine all of these philosophies and techniques.

Shared Experience

Instead of the old "set-up, knock-down" punch line formats, the new greeting cards rely instead on shared experiences and honest, raw feelings to get their laughs.

You can see a similar change if you study the evolution of stand-up comedy. While veteran performers such as Abbott and Costello, George Burns and Jack Benny worked with carefully constructed straight man-vs.-comedian shticks and contrived formula jokes, the "new" comedians (George Carlin, Roseanne Arnold, Louie Anderson, Richard Belzer, Elayne Boosler) get laughs by sharing their own personal, truthful—and funny—experiences. This new, empathetic type of humor is often introduced with a lead-in such as, "Don't you hate it when . . ." or "Have you ever noticed . . ." or "Why is it that. . . ."

On greeting cards, this shared experience humor takes everyday happenings and transforms them into sendable me-to-you messages. Here is an example of shared experience humor:

(OUTSIDE): Help!
(INSIDE): I'm a fudge and truffles person
in a sprouts and tofu world!

Most women are painfully aware of their eating habits and are torn between a lust for thinness and a passion for gooey, sweet, unhealthful foods. This card captures the ambivalence many of us feel about our bodies and the food we eat.

Psychologically speaking, shared experience humor works because the reader feels a resonance or empathy with the humorous situation depicted and described on the card.

In the old days of formulaic greeting card writing, the same type of joke might have looked like this:

(OUTSIDE): Wanted to get you some truffles for your
birthday—
(INSIDE): But my pig overslept.

This card, instead of focusing on shared experience, focuses on the ambiguity of the word "truffles" (expensive chocolates or French mushrooms?).

Direct and Conversational Tone

As with conversational prose, writing the new humor requires you to write the way people talk. More specifically, it requires you to write the way people talk when they kid around or insult each other.

This tone, like the shared experience aspect of new humor, tends to make the cards more intimate than traditional humor cards. Feelings and statements are not veiled in predictable formulas or horrible puns. The message is "out there!" Even semi-rambling sentences are okay if they sound like casual conversation. (It would be nice if we could all communicate like George Will, but in real life that's not usually how we get our ideas across.)

Because women are traditionally more at home with their feelings than men are, this directness makes sense. After all, you're writing to, for and about women. (I realize that I owe an apology to the couple dozen sensitive, in-touch new age men out there. Sorry, guys.)

Here's an example of conversational humor for a birthday card for Dad:

> (OUTSIDE): Dad, I can guarantee you'll never have to worry about *me* writing one of those tell-all books about our family—
>
> (INSIDE): Just leave $300 in small unmarked bills right under your car keys!
>
> P.S. Do exactly as I say or the remote control gets it.
> Happy Birthday

In addition to sounding the way people talk, this card has a shared experience message and also is *topical*; that is, it refers to a timely subject or issue (in this case, tell-all books).

SEX! Now that I have your attention, I just want to *touch* on (pardon the pun) the way sexuality is *handled* in the new humor. Traditional humor tiptoed around sexuality with euphemisms ("May your swash never buckle") and coy compliments ("To the one who makes my pitter patter"). While some suggestive humor made it to the card racks, explicit references to having sex were a big no-no.

Alternative humor cards pull no punches about sex. For most companies, direct references to "having sex" or "good sex" are acceptable. The trend toward super-explicit greeting cards, however, seems to be subsiding. When I create card ideas, I try not to write anything more sexually direct than you might see on late-night talk shows.

Timely Subject Matter

Some new humor is written concerning the trends, fads and happenings in popular culture.

Let's do a little exercise to learn how to make greeting cards out of current events. I am looking at the table of contents of a leading women's magazine. Here are some of the phrases popping out at me:

☛ Briefcase stand-ins

☛ Dress code: business

☛ Don't call it menswear

☛ Pants that relax you

☛ Chronic fatigue syndrome

☛ Is he hooked on lingerie?

☛ Is your nail salon safe?

☛ Stop obsessing about your thighs, hair, breasts

☛ Have you ever shared a look, a touch, a moment of flirtation with a stranger?

☛ Real trust: what couples crave

☛ Why you can't say *no* to dessert

☛ You call this a glamour job?

☛ A renter's guide to decorating

☛ When your friend chooses the wrong man

☛ The truth about prenuptial agreements

☛ Why excuses are healthy

There are even more phrases to choose from — and remember, these have all come from just the table of contents! I will choose three of these phrases and try to brainstorm some new humor cards around each one of them:

#1 Chronic fatigue syndrome

#2 Is your nail salon safe?

#3 A renter's guide to decorating

Let's free associate some words, phrases and sending situations for each potential card.

BRAINSTORM #1 — Chronic Fatigue Syndrome

☛ Chronic fatigue league — Fortieth birthday? New baby?

☛ Platonic fatigue syndrome — lousy love life?

☛ Sleep addiction

☛ Stressed out and tired

CARD IDEAS FROM THIS BRAINSTORM:

(OUTSIDE): Congratulations on your new baby . . .
(INSIDE): . . . and welcome to the Chronic Fatigue
  League!

(OUTSIDE): I've got *so* many guys who want to be my
  friends . . .
(INSIDE): My shrink says I have Platonic Fatigue
  Syndrome!

(OUTSIDE): We're so tired all the time . . .
  maybe it's chronic fatigue syndrome.
(INSIDE): Then again, maybe we're just a couple of
  lethargic old farts.

BRAINSTORM #2 — Is Your Nail Salon Safe?

☛ Tragic nail accident

☛ Cuticles

☛ Sculpted nails

☛ Polish

☛ Frosted polish

CARD IDEA FROM THIS BRAINSTORM:

(OUTSIDE): (character at manicurist): Sorry I haven't
  written . . .
(INSIDE): . . . but I was involved in a tragic nail accident!

BRAINSTORM #3 — A Renter's Guide to Decorating

☛ Shag carpeting/swag lamps

☛ Balconies

☛ Ugly drapes

☛ Mom's old stuff in your first apartment

CARD IDEA FROM THIS BRAINSTORM:

(OUTSIDE): Mom, Even though
I'm grown up, I'm surrounded by
your tender care and loving
concern . . .

(INSIDE): . . . not to mention all the overflow
from your last garage sale!

So you see how it works. Find out what's trendy, brainstorm ways to make topical subjects sendable, then write and rewrite (conversationally!) until you've got some great new humor cards.

The New Slams

Alternative cards have made an art form out of insulting the recipient. The insults are more sarcastic, caustic and blatant than on traditional humor cards.

I'm sure that this mean-spirited form of communication doesn't come naturally to a nice person like you. To get the brutal juices flowing, I try to think of the antagonists I've encountered in various parts of my life: old boyfriends, manipulative co-workers, Robinaires (our high school dance line), boring teachers, domineering bosses, nosy neighbors, smart-ass bureaucrats.

I've mentioned already that writing greeting cards is therapeutic. Think of slams as "anger work." What would you like to say (or like to have said) to those difficult people in your life? Just about anything is fair game: the recipient's age, body, personal habits, love life, clothing, etc.

You can also use celebrities' annoying habits to inspire slams. Turn on the TV. Find a show you hate. What is annoying about the characters on "That Darn Phil"? (They're vapid, obnoxious, and they have the I.Q.s of cereal boxes.) Is there a card there? Maybe. Maybe not.

Here's an example of a good slam for the new humor market:

(OUTSIDE): Excuse me, but as your friend
I feel I have to tell you
that your shoulder pads have slipped
way down around your waist.

(INSIDE): Oops. Those aren't your shoulder pads.
Hang In There!

A second type of slam is the "self-compliment," made famous by Lucy in Charles Schulz's "Peanuts" comic strip. For example:

(OUTSIDE): Happy Birthday to someone
with truly impeccable taste . . .
(INSIDE): . . . in friends!

Because self-compliments are more sendable (they require less intimacy than sending a real humdinger of an insult), they are probably easier for a freelancer to sell than blatant slams.

Insults and self-compliments are fun to write. Be outrageous, blunt, and push them to the limit!

Bizarre Non-Occasion Humor

Another relative newcomer on the humorous greeting card front is the type of card that features a zany cartoon on the cover. These cards often are blank inside, but sometimes they carry a simple me-to-you message. Presumably, people send these cards to share the jokes with their recipients. Gary Larson's "Far Side" is the most notable example of this phenomenon.

This type of humor is *visual*. In fact, many bizarre cartoon cards are spin-offs of comic strips. You will have more success in selling this type of card if you are able to illustrate it yourself or can work with an illustrator.

A Note on Visual Humor

Many of the new humor cards are actually straightforward, generic messages: happy birthday, thinking of you, happy anniversary. The *illustrations* are what push these cards into the alternative category. It is possible for a freelance writer to sell a new humor concept for a simple thinking-of-you message.

Reread Chapter Eight, "Writing Cute and Whimsical Cards," for a refresher on the synergy of design and editorial. Also, "Thinking Visually" in the Workbook section will help you get started.

GREETING CARD PROMOTIONS

In addition to their major alternative lines of cards, some greeting card companies offer small groupings of cards (eight to thirty-two per group) with a unifying design and/or editorial style. These groups of cards are called "promotions," and they often represent the newest and most innovative material out there.

Promotions can be held together in a variety of ways: with a humorous character appearing on all the cards, with a certain target market in mind, with a certain type of writing throughout the promotion, or with an innovative design. Some examples of promotion concepts might be:

- ☛ Original country-music type lyrics illustrated with scenes from the American Southwest.

- ☛ Humorous over-the-hill messages illustrated with whimsical drawings of mischievous children.

- ☛ Quotes from Thoreau and Emerson on the cover with environmental affirmations inside.

- ☛ Humorous birthday and friendship messages for stay-at-home mothers.

Freelancers sometimes can sell concepts for entire promotions. (This, too, is more likely for those gifted people who can both write *and* draw.)

Here's how to develop a promotion concept:

1. Give your concept a working title.

2. Describe your concept in a brief (two- to three-sentence) paragraph.

3. Think of as many sending situations or designs as possible for your promotion concept. Believe me, there's nothing more frustrating than selling a company a promotion concept and then discovering that it won't stretch beyond three or four cards.

4. Contact various companies to determine their policies on accepting promotion concepts. Many companies prefer to add cards one at a time, especially with new

writers and artists. If your individual cards make a company a lot of money, it then becomes easier to sell the company on doing a whole promotion.

5. Beginning with your most enthusiastic editor, submit the concept title, description and mock-ups (complete examples) of several cards. (Submit the cards in the company's preferred format.)

Writing alternative humor is challenging and fun. But be advised that some humor departments have a "more alternative than thou" attitude when it comes to purchasing freelance writing for this market, so try to work for editors who value you as a professional and welcome your contributions.

As a good friend of mine once said, "When creativity stops being fun, it stops being creative." This is especially true of creating humor. So lighten up, have fun, and keep on writing!

CHAPTER TWELVE

The Future of Greeting Cards

$\mathcal{A}$s of this writing, several minitrends are making an impact on the social expression industry. At present the freelance opportunities for these types of products are minimal, but there's a chance that these three areas will be growth areas: non-occasion cards (also known as "anyday" cards), personalized products, and faxed greetings.

NON-OCCASION OR ANYDAY CARDS

We've already learned about many types of non-occasion cards. Long, conversational prose; alternative humor; and even traditional humor and cute cards are often sent for no other reason than to keep in touch.

The newest form of non-occasion (or anyday) card is simple (usually only a sentence or two), conversational, specific and direct. This type of card often (but not always) has a strong design tie-in. Another new wrinkle is that these cards are available not only in general love and friendship captions, but for relatives as well.

Non-occasion is the most experimental area for the big companies, so it's difficult to define. Keep it direct, conversational, and create unique sending situations, and you'll do well.

Think of anyday cards as relationship builders and strengtheners. The messages can be softly confrontal:

> (OUTSIDE): I'm sure you mean well . . .
> (INSIDE): . . . but I need you to let me
>   work this out for myself.

Or they can be simple statements of affection and appreciation between two specific people:

> (OUTSIDE): (illustration of smiling woman):
>   Why is this person smiling?
> (INSIDE): Because she has you for a sister.

Your own life is an excellent source of material for anyday cards. Transform your daily anxieties, regrets and affection into a cleverly worded sentence or two, and your card will be a real winner.

Not all greeting card companies have anyday lines. This signals an opportunity for freelancers. Try presenting a promotion (eight to thirty-two cards, remember?) of anyday cards to companies whose product lines lack these products.

The following idea starters should get your anyday wheels turning:

- ☛ Relationship changes (for better or worse)
- ☛ Family conflicts (confronting or resolving)
- ☛ Social pressures (AIDS, drugs, financial woes)
- ☛ Day-to-day stress (work, parenting, school, aging)
- ☛ Friendship (growing, fading, initiating, ending)

These cards present a fun, creative challenge. What other feelings and thoughts might consumers feel comfortable expressing with a card?

PERSONALIZATION

The phrase "your name here" has graduated from junk mail to greeting cards, thanks to our friend, the computer.

Many Hallmark stores are equipped with computers that can personalize a variety of cards, posters or other products with the recipient's name and other personal information. Undoubtedly, inexpensive technology will enable card stores to offer increasingly sophisticated personalization, and this may become an area of opportunity for freelancers.

When submitting ideas for these cards, think of unique combinations of personalization on each card. For example:

(OUTSIDE): <u>Natalie</u>, everyone here in <u>Lenexa, Kansas</u>,
wants to wish you a happy 29th birthday—
(INSIDE): Even though we all know you're really <u>44</u>!

The following are some other personalization suggestions for cards and other products.

- ☛ Specific anniversary
- ☛ Recipient's name and age
- ☛ Recipient's hometown

☛ Sender's location

☛ Recipients' wedding date

If your computer is equipped with a good graphics package and laser printer, making personalized cards could become a fun and lucrative hobby for you.

Here's how to get started:

1. Using the skills acquired in this book, develop a file of card writing for all sending situations. Include humorous, general and juvenile ideas — verse and prose.

2. Illustrate these ideas.

3. Make a customer catalog of your card ideas — one card per page.

4. Starting with your own friends and family, begin sending personalized cards for birthdays and other occasions.

5. Place an ad in the newspaper (or sign in the supermarket) to solicit new customers. If your cards are good, word-of-mouth advertising will make your business grow.

We all like to see our names in print. Personalized greeting cards single out recipients on special occasions and give them the attention they deserve.

FAX GREETINGS

Most businesses and many homes are now equipped with fax machines. This suggests another opportunity for sending greetings.

Business-to-business thank-yous, introductions and announcements can be communicated instantly and inexpensively using fax technology.

Examples of fax greetings might be:

(Illustration of moving van full of animated numbers and dollar signs):

Bob Smith Accounting has moved!
New Address:

or

(Illustration of character swinging and missing with
    baseball bat):
We Missed Your Payment!
Please remit _____ at your earliest convenience.

Editors and creative directors are impressed when writers are aware of what's happening in the industry. Your job as a freelancer is not only to keep up with greeting card trends; the most successful social expression writers *anticipate* trends. And once you get rolling, who knows? You may be setting those trends yourself.

Self-Expression Products

CHAPTER THIRTEEN

"Kiss Me — I'm Whatever!"
OR

Writing for Self-Expression Products

$\int$ elf-expression writing is what you'll find on most social expression products that *aren't* cards. At Hallmark, we called these items "specialty products," and they include T-shirts, bumper stickers, buttons and mugs. Other companies have other names for these products: "novelties," "allied products" or simply "gifts."

Writing for self-expression products almost always has a me-to-the-rest-of-the-world message (in contrast with the me-to-you messages on greeting cards).

Some familiar examples of this are:

- ☛ I ♥ MY FERRET (or *pit bull, bass boat*, etc.)!
- ☛ BABY (or *square dancer, dieter*, etc.) ON BOARD!
- ☛ I'D RATHER BE SAILING (or *shopping, networking*, etc.)!

Self-expression writing is about as much fun as you can have in this business without wearing a hat! People love to express themselves with everything from the very zany to the most inspirational of messages. It's great fun to discover that a bumper sticker you created out of your own experience strikes a chord with other people, and that they decide to buy it and stick it on their very own cars!

THE SELF-EXPRESSION PRODUCT MARKET

Although this market, like greeting cards, is predominantly feminine (more than 90 percent), the purchasers tend to be a little younger, a little hipper, and more tuned in to humor—much like the buyers of alternative cards.

The major buying difference is that about half of self-expression products are purchased for oneself, and the other half as gifts. (If greeting cards aren't used 100 percent as gifts, there must be some poor souls out there buying them and sending them to themselves!)

Another difference to keep in mind is that while greeting cards are a private means of communication, posters, buttons and T-shirts are displayed publicly. For this reason, the feelings and thoughts communicated on self-expression products are less intimate than those expressed on cards.

In this chapter, we'll look at the major self-expression products and practice creating copy for each. Then, in Chapter Fifteen, you'll find information on how and where to sell all this terrific writing.

Mugs

Many social expression and gift companies produce mugs with self-expression copy and designs. Consequently, there's room for lots of innovation, humor and target marketing.

When writing copy for self-expression products, begin by asking, "Who uses this product, and where?" A list of mug-using situations might look like this:

WORKPLACE	HOME
Men	Mom
Women	Dad
Secretaries	Husband
Bosses	Wife
Career specific — lawyers, doctors, nurses, accountants, teachers, computer programmers, etc.	

Next, think of the types of messages that might work on mugs in those settings.

WORKPLACE	SUBJECT MATTER
Men	Sports, sex, achievement
Women	Stress, men, fashion, weight
Secretaries	Overworked/underpaid
Bosses	Compliments/tyranny humor
Career specific	Humor/inspiration related to specific occupations

HOME	SUBJECT MATTER
Mom	Stress, kids, love, friendship, working mom/stay-at-home mom, motherhood, new mom, budgets, housework
Dad	Sports, handyman, funny clothes, couch potato, snacks, kids
Husband	Sex, partnership, love
Wife	Sex, love, budgets, dieting

Now I'll take you through the writing process, as we mentally combine the mug-using situations with the subject matter. You will recognize writing tricks from Chapter Two. I've italicized the usable material.

What message about housework might a mom like on her mug? Let's see . . . dirty dishes, vacuuming, dusting, dust bunnies. What about a scary rabbit wearing an apron—*The Mother of All Dust Bunnies*. I like it. Ironing. Pumping Iron? Dumping Iron? I went through four years of college for this? How about *I got stretch marks for this?* The illustration could be a mom tied up by toddlers or cleaning spaghetti off the ceiling. By the way, where are my kids? They're awfully quiet. *Has anybody seen my kids?* I love it.

We've strayed from housework to motherhood, and that's okay. Let your mind jump back and forth and write down everything that hits you as catchy or funny.

Another way to write for self-expression products is to write about the product itself: in this case, write a mug *about* mugs.

Let's create together again:

What do people use mugs for? For coffee, mostly. Why? Because they need caffeine. How about a militant woman? *My husband, sure. My house, maybe. My caffeine, never.* Some people drink decaf. Decaf. People nag me about drinking real coffee. What would get them off my case? *It's okay. It's decaf.* How about a mug for the disciples of decaffeination? *Decaffeinate or Die.* How about caffeine addiction? *The Queen of Caffeine.*

The preceding examples all are in a humorous vein. Complimentary and inspirational (even religious) copy, too, are suitable for mugs. Again, the creative process:

What kind of mug might a traditionally oriented woman give to a lifelong friend? *God Bless Our Coffee Break*. Friends. Friends are forever. *Friends Are the Sweetener in the Coffee of Life*. Maybe an illustration of two cute animals having coffee. *World's Greatest Listener*.

Think of mugs as bumper stickers for the desk or kitchen. Other markets to brainstorm are graduation, retirement, sister, grandmother, and across the miles.

As when writing alternative greeting cards, magazines can be helpful in suggesting subject matter and tone for mugs. When writing mugs for Mom, browse through a *Parent's* or *Family Circle* magazine. For Dad, try *Sports Illustrated*. And so on. The world is your library when researching social expression products.

Posters

Posters are vehicles through which consumers make a statement at home, school or office. The tone can range from inspiring ("I have a dream . . .") to complaining ("My other house is a dump, too.").

I believe there are actually *two* distinct poster markets:

Teenage Market

Subject matter for these flashy posters includes rock stars, hunks, bikinis and muscle cars. The bigger the image, the better! The visual pizzazz is the main draw for this market.

Writers with photographic skills will have the edge in selling this type of poster copy. Companies are often more interested when a creator can provide both words and pictures, especially in visual products such as posters.

But even if you've never held a camera, you can create your own photo-plus-words posters. You can purchase stock photographs in most large cities. (Look in the Yellow Pages under "Photography.") Photographers and models sell their work to photo agencies to supplement their other income. For about fifty dollars and up, you can purchase negatives and the rights to publish those negatives as you wish.

When we were writing mugs, the words came first, then the design ideas. For posters, the image is everything; so we need to start with the visual.

Let's say we have procured the rights to a photo of a desirable young man leaning across the hood of a sleek black Corvette. Our market here, primarily, would be teenage girls. Let's start our creative process again. What statement does a poster like this make for teenage girls? What words come to mind?

Dream come true. Hot hunks of love. Prince Charming. Mr. Right. A few good men. We're looking for a few good men. *I'm looking for a few good men*. No. *I'm looking for a few bad boys*. I've got my fantasies to keep me warm. Welcome to Fantasyland. *You can tell men from boys by the price of their toys*. Fantasies. *Fantasy wanted. Experience required.*

Home or Office Humor/Inspiration Market

Market number two is composed of slightly older people and definitely smaller posters. Look for your purchasers to be in the eighteen-to-thirty-five age range, mostly women. They'll buy some inspiration, some religious, and a lot of humor for offices, homes and college dorm rooms.

Because the humor or inspiration is the focus for this market, we'll start with the words. What humorous poster would a twenty-year-old secretary want displayed in her workspace? Let's create:

Stress. Busy. *Not now—I'm busy* (with drawing of secretary watching soaps or filing nails). Efficiency. *I'm too cute to be efficient*. Unreasonable employers. Bosses. Underpaid. Overworked. Emergency. *No reasonable emergency ignored.*

Let's say this same secretary is a devout Christian mom who wants to display some words of wisdom and faith in her home. What would she want a kitchen poster to say? This time let's start with a biblical verse and brainstorm whimsical illustrations to accompany it.

> "A new commandment I give to you,
> that you love one another;
> even as I have loved you."
>
> John 13:34

This could be illustrated with a little girl helping a younger sister. Or a sweet drawing of a mother and child. Or a child putting a bandage on a doll.

Whether you start with a visual image, your own clever words, or a literary or biblical quotation, creating posters — matching powerful words with powerful pictures — is a fun and challenging part of being a social expression writer.

Plaques

Think of plaques as being eight-dollar greeting cards. They almost always are purchased as gifts. Plaques were right at home in the sixties and seventies ("You are you and I am I, and if by chance we find each other, it's groovy"), but fewer companies have success with plaques in the nineties.

Friendship and inspiration are the strongest captions for the plaque market.

Religious bookstores have the most extensive selections of plaques at present, no doubt due to the timelessness of those messages for Christians. You can get the names and addresses of plaque manufacturers from shop owners, then write to inquire about freelance opportunities. (Review chapter six on religious and inspirational writing.)

WARNING: Humorous plaques — probably because of the high price — are not a good bet. You're better off sticking to general prose or verse. Biggest captions: *friendship*, *inspiration*, *love*, mother, *sister*, *grandmother*, *teacher* and *new baby*.

Ornaments and Figurines

Keep it traditional, keep it short, and date it with the year if you can. Ornaments and figurines are, for the most part, collectible and commemorative.

It's no surprise that the big season for ornaments is Christmas. But it might surprise you to know that even in the middle of the summer, the vendors in the Orient are unable to keep up with the demand of the consumers. (So *that's* why many card shops start displaying their ornaments right after Father's Day!)

Ornaments are both highly appropriate for gifts and highly collectible (and collectors probably are in the self-purchase category). This means an emphasis on specific captions, such as *baby's first Christmas, first Christmas together, mother, father, grandmother, grandfather, aunt, sister, teacher* — you get the idea. Shop a well-stocked ornament display and take notes.

If you can draw, your odds of selling an ornament are greatly increased. Some ornaments are sculpted in the Orient from sketches by artists at companies such as Hallmark.

It is possible to write packaging copy — usually a cute quotation or poem — on assignment. Social expression companies recognize that special words can increase the perceived value and collectibility of ornaments.

Figurines are both an everyday and seasonal collectible item. Copy is usually very short (due to limited space on the figurine) and very safe (due to the relatively high price of ceramic figurines): "Follow your dreams," "look to this day," "friends are forever" — that kind of thing.

When I was on Hallmark's writing staff, we used to joke that it would be nice to have some "word dice" for creating this type of copy. One of the dice would have inspirational verbs, such as *follow, believe in* and *listen to*. The other would have inspirational nouns, such as *rainbow, heart,* and *dreams*. Then, simply by rolling the dice, we'd fill in the blanks of the following piece of figurine copy:

_____ YOUR _____

Follow your dreams	Follow your heart
Listen to your dreams	Listen to your heart
Believe in your dreams	Believe in your heart

Follow your rainbow

Listen to your rainbow

Believe in your rainbow

This is a fun exercise, but it won't make you rich, because no company is going to pay money for such generic copy.

A freelancer's best bet is to work with an artist and create a concept for a group of ornaments for a specific target market.

EXAMPLE: You've decided to create a family of figurines for traditional, nature-loving consumers. What types of characters will you include? Woodland characters have been done over and over again. Kittens and puppies, though traditionally best-selling subject matter, don't reflect "nature" as much as they do "home" or "friendship."

What if the artist designed soft, cute stylings of endangered wildlife? This kind of material would be highly marketable in our ecologically conscious times.

What copy would you use? Let's try to think of simple ecological messages: *Give nature a hug. All things bright and beautiful. Love your neighbor.* (With cute animals — a real tear-jerker.)

As with plaques, ornament and figurine manufacturers' addresses are readily available in gift and card shops. Just make sure you can provide a concept, design direction and copy that sets your product line apart from the others.

Calendars

Whether it's a wall calendar with twelve or thirteen different designs and support copy, a week-at-a-glance desk calendar, or a 365-page-a-day calendar, a calendar requires a strong, unifying concept or theme to pull it together.

Wall calendars are basically visual, so the look needs to be beautiful, funny, cute, nostalgic, sexy, dramatic, etc. To sell a calendar idea, think of a strong concept, write a proposal describing the concept in a paragraph or two, and explain why the look you're proposing needs the support and enhancement of your copy. For example, if your concept is "Doo-Wop Groups of the Fifties," you must show that your biographic and discographic information and your stellar writing style are absolutely essential in pulling the whole idea together. You will also need to create two or three sample months showing *exactly* what you have in mind.

Week-at-a-glance calendars need to be functional. Don't let your concept or theme distract you or the purchaser from the functionality of the calendar. (For example, if you submitted an idea for a Music Lover's Calendar, each week might have a quotation from a famous musician. But don't make the quotation or illustration too big, or the calendar's function is diminished.)

If you sell a concept for a 365-page-a-day calendar, be sure you (1) have a reasonable editor, and (2) have no life other than the writing of this calendar. It is very difficult, especially for a freelancer, to get an editor to purchase 365 pieces of copy. I wrote a humorous page-a-day calendar in 1985. By the time I'd written enough copy to satisfy my editor and her boss and her boss's boss, I figure I made about three dollars per joke. This is roughly equal to the hourly wage I earned assembling cheese steak sandwiches at DeVito's Delicatessen in 1975, except that DeVito's provided a uniform and free lunches.

However, having your name on a calendar is exciting. You get to know that your words of humor or wisdom helped someone through a whole year. And it's an impressive addition to your social expression portfolio.

T-Shirts, Sweatshirts and Nightshirts

These products are near the top of every writer's fun list. They're like bumper stickers for the body. The world is your inspiration. Almost any topic on the Self-Expression Idea Starter page in the Workbook section should give you dozens of ideas.

The T-shirt market is both self-purchase and gift oriented. Target markets and specific captions are good places to start in creating T-shirt ideas.

Because the consumer actually wears the message (unlike mugs, posters, plaques and calendars), the me-to-the-rest-of-the-world message must be attention-getting and clever.

Let's try to write some T-shirt copy. Our consumer wants a gift for a forty-something male golf nut. What should that shirt say? Again, let's spell out the brainstorming process. First, what are some good golf words?

IDEAS: Tee. Drive. *Golfers do it while they're driving*. Stroke. Putt. 19th hole. Hole in one. Cheating on scorecard. *Hidden Hills Country Club Creative Scorekeeping Champion*. Golf pants. Golf shoes. Golf balls. Lie. Bad lie. Fairway. U.S. Open. P.G.A. Putting. *King of the Three-Putt*. Swearing. *Golfers Swear at Their Balls*.

As you can see, despite the specific constraints of various product formats, the creative *process* remains basically the same for all self-expression product lines. Incidentally, when you hit on a particularly strong copy idea, try plugging it in to different products. "King of the Three-Putt," for example, could also work on a coffee mug, key ring or button.

T-shirt copy ideas can be marketed to social expression companies (look in shirt stores to see who makes them).

As with other products, if you can provide your own design, you can try to manufacture and sell them yourself. (If you do and you become a millionaire, don't forget where you got the idea!)

Another approach is to license your design (on a royalty basis) to a social expression or T-shirt company.

Chapter Fifteen discusses the relative advantages and disadvantages of these methods of marketing self-expression products.

Bumper Stickers

Bumper stickers might be called the granddaddy of all self-expression. There's a certain zealous, compulsive confederation of people (one of whom I'm married to) who have an overwhelming need to communicate their deepest and most personal feelings and beliefs to the rest of the innocent souls on the planet.

I'd love to see some marketing wizard try to zero in on the timeless popularity of this product. Let me take a stab at it, and I won't even charge you two million dollars, or whatever the going rate is. The bumper sticker market is made up of people who are slightly insecure. They're looking for kindred souls (or kindred cars), and their bumper messages are a semi-anonymous, nonthreatening way to communicate who they are and what they believe.

Spin-offs of old formulas work well with bumper stickers. For example, first you'll see a bumper sticker that says, "Have a nice day." Then a few months later you'll see one that says, "Have an average day." Then you'll see another that says, "Have a nice day somewhere else."

Let's practice writing bumper stickers. This time, let's use the forced writing trick mentioned in Chapter Two. I'm going to give myself two minutes to write all the bumper stickers I can. (You'll have to trust me. What choice do you have? Okay. It's 10:01. Ready, set, go!)

My other car is a spaceship. Save the planet. Shave the planet. All mothers are working mothers. Mom's taxi. Mom's limo. I ♥ my cholesterol. Souvenir of Hell. Rock-and-roll mom on board. I never met a hunk I didn't like.

There. 10:03. Not volumes of bumper stickers, but a start. Now you try it. No cheating.

If you have a computer that produces camera-ready artwork, you may be able to market these yourself. The "Advertising Specialties" classification in the Yellow Pages includes the names of printers who print bumper stickers.

Keep alert to what's going on with these fun and diverse self-expression products, but don't tailgate!

(P.S. If you don't like my writing, call 1-800-SO SUE ME.)

Buttons

Whether we're kids, teenagers, young adults or "mature" grown-ups, most of us like the attention and smiles a clever button can bring our way.

Due to the necessarily small type size, button messages can be more risqué than bumper sticker or T-shirt copy. We can assume that our consumers have fairly close relationships with those who can read the fine print on their chests.

Keep it short. Timely or trendy copy is great for buttons. Sometimes flipping product formats can be fun. "Honk if you're horny" is an old bumper sticker, but it might make a cute button. Buttons that invite interaction between the wearer and the viewer ("Kiss me, I'm Elvis," "Wink if you're available," etc.) are also good possibilities.

Once again, we're going to create some copy together. This time, as a mental challenge, I'm going to write buttons suitable to be worn by my evil twin; that is, by the hypothetical consumer out there whose politics, values, opinions and interests are 180 degrees away from my own.

Let's see. What buttons might the other Molly find amusing? Barefoot, pregnant and fulfilled. Take me to your sports bar. (With a Martian illustration, that could be funny.) Aerobics is my life. Chief cook and bottle washer. You call that music? Perfect specimen. In your dreams. I ♥ the Contras.

This is an excellent marketing exercise, because it reminds me that

I am not necessarily representative of the entire social expression market. Try it with *your* evil twin.

As with bumper stickers, many printers have facilities for manufacturing buttons, should you decide to market them yourself. Again, look under "Advertising Specialties" in the Yellow Pages.

Checkbook Covers, Key Rings and Combs

"Self-expression for the purse" is a growing product group. You can find these products in most card shops as well as drug stores, discount houses and gift shops. Ask the proprietors for the names and addresses of manufacturers.

Checkbook covers have become vehicles of social expression because people like to kid about how broke they are or how ineptly they handle their finances. "My other account is solvent." See? It's a spin-off of an old bumper sticker. Maybe the humor on the cover helps cope with the pain of paying bills. Shopping, food, budget and office are also possible topics for checkbook cover humor.

Key ring humor is very similar to bumper sticker humor. Car-related ideas are strong, as are general humor and inspiration.

Combs and comb/mirror sets are geared toward the teenage market. The copy tends to be vanity-related ("Nice Face!") and young-sounding ("Awesome dude!")

Car Window Signs

The suction cup has given new life and new domain to the field of automotive communication. Everything that applies to bumper stickers applies here. Beware, though, because these little gimmicks may be more of a flash-in-the-pan fad than a trend.

New Product Ideas

Most companies that market self-expression products are always on the lookout for new product ideas and line extensions. An example of a line extension idea would be a group of tiny suction cup signs that stick on your eyeglasses. (I didn't say a *good* example.) So the basic product line would be suction cup signs; the line extension would be minisuction cup eyeglass signs.

Submitting and protecting these ideas can be tricky. If you have a new product idea, it's best to work with a company and an editor with whom you've established a good, strong, trustworthy relationship. Chapter Fifteen includes information on protecting your creative ideas.

The Bad News

One unfortunate note: Because self-expression writing is so much fun, everybody likes to do it. And because of the laws of supply and demand—because everybody likes to do it—companies generally don't pay as much for self-expression as for other types of writing. (My own experience has been anywhere from $20 to $100 for a perfectly wonderful piece of self-expression product writing.) Writers must be creative and persistent in marketing their ideas.

The New York Stationery Show is the number one trade show for the entire social expression industry. Almost every greeting card and self-expression product company in the business is represented. Incredibly, more than eight hundred exhibitors have booths at the show. (You can find many potential clients there.) You'll also find dozens of different formats for self-expression products.

Two monthly social expression trade publications, *Greetings* magazine and *Gifts and Decorative Accessories*, feature new products from leading manufacturers. Subscribing to these would be worthwhile to any aspiring self-expression writers.

Remember, to succeed at self-expression writing, all you have to do is dream up some new, exciting, marketable way for people to tell the world how they feel. Or think of a product that is so highly original, provocative and desirable that consumers will just *have* to spring up off their couches and go buy it.

Who knows? You could be sitting on the next Pet Rock.

Selling
Your
Writing

CHAPTER FOURTEEN

"Where Do Ideas Come From?"
OR

Building an Idea
Starter File

The Workbook section of this book includes idea starter pages for each of the major greeting card occasions. These word lists will help you get started when you sit down to write.

But it's equally valuable to become an "idea sponge" as you go through your daily routine. With a little practice, you can learn to be open to the stimulation and inspiration that surround you every day.

IDEA SOURCES

Personal Experience

Greeting cards are all about communication. Use your interactions with your family, friends and co-workers to spark ideas for new messages and card sending situations.

Having a feud with your in-laws? What emotions are behind that conflict? Can you write a card about it? Can you make it funny?

Bouncing checks this month? Turn that negative experience into a positive. Write some checkbook covers or some shared experience cards.

Are your kids using silly and/or naughty words? Can you turn the experience into a juvenile card? Maybe you can even create a character based on your own child.

Even when you're not actually working, you can gather material for cards. I sometimes carry a pack of self-stick notes in my pocket and jot the idea starters down as I think of them.

Books and Magazines

As I demonstrated in Chapter Eleven, magazines, especially women's magazines, are wonderful sources of raw material for cards. Both humorous and serious sending situations are suggested in the types of articles the magazines run.

For example, an article titled "Why Some Girls Never Grow Up" could be the source of material for father birthday, sister birthday, mother birthday, or non-occasion cards for family members or friends. Remember that the best cards — humorous and serious — are those based on honest feelings.

What are the titles on the *New York Times* best-seller list? What sociological phenomena cause those books to be popular? What kinds of greeting cards or self-expression products might push those same sociological buttons?

TV and Movies

Cable TV and feature films are real assets to a freelance card writer. What better way to keep up with the trends that drive popular culture? Train your mind to think of these types of entertainment as sources for your ideas.

What does the success of this year's hot TV series suggest for the greeting card industry? Is there a way to put that phenomenon into social expression?

Who are the guests on this week's talk shows? What do women experience *today* that might drive them to buy a card?

The Social Expression Industry

As you can guess, it is very important to stay on top of the trends in the greeting card business. Before submitting cards to any client, you should have a good idea of what the company's line looks and sounds like, as well as what might be areas of growth for that company.

PLAGIARISM AND COPYRIGHT LAW

Your reputation as a freelancer will quickly be destroyed if you submit card ideas that you've "researched" from other creators. Never, *ever* plagiarize. Remember that greeting card editors and creative directors know what's out there—not only in their own lines, but throughout the industry. Besides, it's more fun to create something of your own.

Similarly, for any product you think up, manufacture, and market yourself, be careful to respect existing copyrights. Celebrities own the right to determine how and where their images are displayed and what their images will advertise. They expect, and have a right, to pick and choose (and be quite handsomely paid for) the use of the fame they've worked so hard to achieve. Clint Eastwood may not be excited that you've put his picture on a coffee mug with the sentiment "Make My Day." And you certainly don't want Clint Eastwood annoyed at you, do you?

Even fictional characters, from Snow White to Miss Piggy, are usually copyrighted and often fiercely protected from unauthorized use by others who have neither paid for the privilege nor been approved by the copyright holder. Finding Papa Smurf pictured in a compromising position with Olive Oyl, or on your knee-slappingly funny personalized toilet tissue, may be less than amusing to the heirs of those characters' creators and bring you results you never intended.

If you're absolutely determined to feature a prominent cartoon character on the car window hang-up you're peddling outside your local cineplex, you may, in some cases, be able to reach a licensing agreement with the copyright holder. This would probably allow you the use of the image for a percentage of what you make from the sale. It's expensive, and the paperwork can be considerable, but you're welcome to try.

If you *don't* secure the right to use a copyrighted image but use it anyway, be warned that your charming self-expression products, and all the money you've made from them, can be forfeited, and that you can be sued, besides, for copyright infringement. That's trouble nobody needs and you definitely don't want. So especially when you're beginning, use your own slogans, your own ideas, and your own (or your partner's) drawings. Avoid ideas based on existing characters, fictional or otherwise.

ASSEMBLING YOUR RESEARCH FILES

Let's face it: Some days, a writer just doesn't feel like writing. You can turn that down time into productive time by using it for research.

Here's a good method for starting a research file:

1. Start with ten file folders. Label them as follows:

Birthday	Juvenile
Feminine relatives	Miscellaneous humor
Masculine relatives	Visual ideas
Woman-to-woman issues	Inspirational
Woman-to-man issues	Seasonal ideas

2. Flip through current magazines and newspapers. Tear out interesting concepts, phrases, visuals and articles. As you file them in the appropriate folder, jot notes on index cards or self-stick notes suggesting ways of transforming this raw material into greeting cards and other social expression products.

3. As you get new ideas from other sources (your relationships, work, nature, TV, movies), jot them down and file them in these same folders.

4. When your writing energy returns (whenever that may be), flip through these files. You'll be amazed at how many card ideas you've assembled.

5. As you receive requests for different types of writing, and as you become aware of new social trends and movements, create new files. Before you know it, your file cabinets will be bulging with creative fodder.

CHAPTER FIFTEEN

"Getting It Going, Keeping It Going"

OR

The Business of Social Expression Writing

Now you have the know-how to write cards like a pro. You probably have shoe boxes full of ideas or half-ideas just waiting to be sold. But remember: *Sold* is the key word. When you market your greeting card ideas, you are in *sales*. And like all salespeople, you must do everything possible to cultivate and maintain the goodwill and respect of your customers.

Here are some valuable tips for getting started and staying organized and motivated as a freelance writer in the social expression industry:

Set Up Your Workspace

Find a private, cheerful, quiet spot to establish your freelance writing business. Surround yourself with information: You need shelf space for your dictionary, rhyming dictionary, thesaurus, magazines and industry publications. You also need file cabinets (one to start) for organizing your research files and information from clients.

Treat Yourself to Office Supplies

The following are essential for setting up shop: manila folders, nine-by-twelve-inch envelopes, business-sized envelopes, postage scale, stamps, stapler, tape, paper clips, self-stick notes, index cards (three-by-five and/or four-by-six), pens, pencils, and address book or Rolodex for keeping track of clients.

Optional office supplies are: wipe-off wallboard (with dry-erase markers) for keeping track of assignments and submissions, printed business cards and stationery, and a week-at-a-glance calendar.

Make Friends With Technology

My own business could not survive without my home computer and fax and answering machines.

A computer streamlines the writing process and simplifies record keeping. A laser or ink jet printer is necessary if you intend to produce your own camera-ready "typesetting" for products. (Most social expression companies will accept dot matrix printed submissions, however.)

A fax machine enables you to provide quicker turnaround to regular clients. The social expression companies I work with are located all over the country, and I've found that my fax has helped me strengthen old relationships and cultivate new ones. If possible, have a separate phone line exclusively for fax use.

Answering machines, voice mail or answering services are essential for freelancers. Clients cannot give you assignments if they can't reach you. They'll simply get in touch with another freelancer who's more available than you are.

Establish a Realistic Work Routine and Stick to It

Lack of structure is both the friend and the enemy of the freelancer. If you are to succeed, you must discipline yourself to do your work reliably and punctually. It's not like having an office job. No boss will check up on you. No secretary will remind you of your obligations. It's all up to you. (Have a nice day—and stay out of the refrigerator!)

Now you're all set up. It's time to start building your client base.

SELLING WRITING TO A COMPANY

Research the Markets

If you plan to sell writing to a company, obtain a current copy of the *Greeting Card Industry Directory*. (See the Greeting Card Writer's Library, page 192.) This gold mine of names, addresses and information is published biannually for the National Stationery Show in New York. The directory also includes detailed lists of each company's product lines, including novelty products.

The current year's *Writer's Market*, too, is a necessity before getting started. The section on greeting card publishers provides names, titles, addresses, phone numbers and general guidelines for each company listed.

Study the books and make a list of contacts at the companies whose product lines match your interests and talents. Make a file folder for each company you intend to contact. Fill each folder with notes and, if possible, product samples procured from your local social expression shop. The files will keep your correspondence and follow-up information handy and organized.

Letters of Introduction

Write letters of introduction to the top ten contacts on your list. (For clarity's sake, I will call these contacts "editors," although they may have

SAMPLE INTRODUCTION LETTER:

Mr. Card
Submissions Editor
Monolith Greetings
Midwestern City, Midwestern State

Dear Mr. Card,

   I am most interested in developing a freelance writing relationship with Monolith. I am sending a résumé to give you an idea of my background and abilities.

   I have also enclosed a self-addressed, stamped envelope. Please send me a copy of your latest needs and guidelines.

   May I phone you next week to discuss freelance opportunities and procedures? I'm looking forward to talking with you and, I hope, working with you.

Sincerely,

Not just another greeting card writer

a slightly different title, such as "freelance coordinator," "creative director," or even "art director.") Be polite, friendly, enthusiastic and original. (See sample letter above.) If you have any experience in writing or editing, enclose a résumé. Printed business cards tend to enhance your professional image.

Let each editor know when you'll follow up with a phone call.

Follow-Up Phone Calls

If you, like many writers (myself included), are shy and have stage fright about talking to strangers on the phone, remember: Almost everyone in the greeting card industry is *nice*. (Sadistic people tend to gravitate toward other fields, such as dentistry and driver's license examining.)

   Jot down several good questions to ask your editors. What percentage of their writing do they purchase from freelancers? What is their preferred submission format—index cards, typed sheets, or folded card blanks? How often do they review freelance material? Is there any type of material they *don't* need? Do they accept faxed submissions?

By now you should have studied this company's line. Let the editor know that you've done your homework.

> EXAMPLE: I bought one of your buttons the other day—
> "Vacuuming sucks." It looks like you're trying
> some off-the-wall approaches.

You want your editors to think of you as a person, not just as a name on a résumé. Also, if possible, you want your editors to *like* you personally. This means you must continually walk that fine line between being friendly and being a pest.

Now you're ready to call. Take a deep breath, dial the number, and put on your best, most confident greeting card writer/salesperson voice.

The following examples may be helpful in preparing for those first few calls:

> BAD FORM: "I'm always writing funny little cards for my
> friends and family, and they all think I'm
> hysterical. Can I send you some stuff?"
> GOOD FORM: "Hello, my name is Helen Steiner Rice (or
> whatever), and I'm a greeting card writer.
> I've admired your products and would
> like very much to contribute some
> writing."

From my experience both at Hallmark and freelancing for other clients, I've come to believe that the goodwill you generate with your clients can really boost your sales. And, conversely, being overly pushy or overly sensitive to criticism can diminish your success with *any* client.

Work for Hire

When purchasing "work for hire" (that is, writing sold for a flat one-time fee; no royalties), most companies require contributors to sign a release form *before* submitting ideas. This routine document spells out the company's policy on copyrights and royalties and protects the company in case of duplicate submissions.

SUBMISSIONS

Submit your ideas in the format and quantity requested, accompanied by a friendly cover note reminding the editor who you are. The following are general guidelines for submitting various product writing to social expression companies:

Submitting Greeting Card Copy

If your editor requests submissions on three-by-five or four-by-six index cards:

- ☛ Put one typewritten idea on each card.
- ☛ Type the caption, occasion, and/or season in the upper left-hand corner.
- ☛ Specify which lines of copy go on the outside and which go on the inside of the card. If necessary, describe the illustration you envision for the cover.

The submission below has been set up in this format.

If your editor requests submissions on 8½ × 11-inch sheets, use the same "outside-inside" style as for the index cards format. However, put no more than two submissions on each sheet.

General Friendship

(OUTSIDE):
(illustration of upside-down opossum):
Hi!
(INSIDE):
How's it hangin'?

If your editor requests ideas submitted in "mock-up" form:

☞ Fold an 8½ × 11-inch sheet of paper in half. Type one card idea on each folded sheet.

☞ Type the caption, occasion, and/or season in the upper left-hand corner of the cover.

☞ Obviously, you will type the cover copy and optional design suggestions on the cover. (If you can draw, illustrating the cover of your card enhances its presentation.) The typed inside copy goes on the inside.

Submitting Greeting Card Promotion Concepts

Presentation is everything when you're trying to sell a company a whole group of your cards.

Accompany submissions with a letter stating the concept behind your group of cards. Support your proposal with any market information or design direction you can provide, as in the sample letter on page 155.

You should include no fewer than three specific card ideas, submitted in the format (index cards, 8½ × 11-inch sheets, or mock-ups) preferred by the company you're approaching. Include artwork, too, if available.

Submitting Self-Expression Product Copy

When offering your one-liners for a self-expression editor's consideration, it's to your advantage to have each idea looked at *by itself*. Submitting columns of one-liners on a typed sheet invites a cursory look by an editor or approval committee. For this reason, unless your editor specifies otherwise, index cards are the best format for submitting self-expression copy ideas.

1. Type the product category and season or occasion in the upper left-hand corner of each card.

2. As with greeting card submissions, give design direction (in parentheses) when necessary.

The following submission has been set up in this format:

St. Patrick's Day
Button

(show funny parade float)
Blarney on Board

Whenever You Submit *Any* Idea to a Social Expression Company . . .

1. If an editor asks for batches of ten cards at a time, send *ten*. Even if you have stacks of material to submit, pace yourself. Remember, you want to keep him or her wanting more.

2. Make sure that your name, address and telephone number are on the back of each idea you submit.

3. Devise a numbering system for your submissions. This helps you keep track of which ideas are circulating where. It also enables your editors to send you a simple note — "We're buying numbers four, six, and seven" — to inform you of their decisions to purchase.

4. *Always* enclose a self-addressed, stamped envelope for the return of your rejects (or, to use a euphemism coined by my former Hallmark boss, Gordon MacKenzie, "not-yet-used-ideas"). If your submissions are on index cards or typed sheets, a business-sized envelope is fine. If your cards are submitted in mock-up form, you'll need a larger envelope.

5. Simultaneous submissions — identical ideas sent to more than one company at the same time — are a no-no in this business. It's too confusing for everybody involved.

6. Know how to protect ownership of your work. Become familiar with copyright law. As of 1978, original works are protected by copyright from the moment of their creation. This copyright extends for the length

SAMPLE CONCEPT PROMOTION LETTER:

Ms. Card
Submissions Editor
Monolith Greetings
Midwestern City, Midwestern State

Dear Ms. Card,

I have developed a greeting card promotion group titled "Earth Kids." The cards (printed on recycled paper) will depict cute children doing nature-loving tasks: planting trees, watering flowers, feeding a squirrel, picking up litter, and looking at the clouds.

The messages on the card will range from general friendship ("Take Care") to gentle ecological reminders ("Love nature like she loves us").

I think the promotion has great potential in our ecologically aware times. Its message could become even more meaningful if a percentage of profits were donated to Sierra Club or another environmental organization.

I hope you'll consider this concept for inclusion in Monolith's promotion offering.

Sincerely,

A greeting card writer aware of current trends

of the creator's life plus fifty years. (Those works copyrighted before 1978 are also automatically protected under the new statute, except for those works already in the public domain.)

As owner of the copyright, you have the exclusive rights of reproduction, sale, public display and distribution of your work.

You should add a copyright notice (typed or handwritten) on the front or back of each piece of writing you submit. This notice is not legally necessary (your work is protected by copyright with or without the notice), but it demonstrates to your clients that you are aware of your rights under copyright law. The correct form for a copyright notice is "Copyright," or "Copr.," or the letter "c" in a circle; your name; and the year of first publication. "Publication," under the 1978 law, means the year when you first publicly distributed or submitted this piece of writing.

Registering a copyright with the U.S. Copyright Office is not necessary to ensure copyright protection. But if your copyright is infringed, no statutory damages or attorney's fees can be paid unless the copyright has been registered.

You can obtain a free Copyright Information Kit by writing to the Copyright Office, Library of Congress, Washington, D.C. 20559.

7. Keep careful track of where your ideas are circulating at all times. If three weeks pass and you haven't heard from a particular editor, call to ask the status of your submissions.

The following is a sample record-keeping sheet for social expression submissions. The writer submitted ten ideas (numbered 1-1 through 1-10) to Hallmark on August 4, 1992. Two ideas (numbers 1-1 and 1-9) were purchased. Hallmark paid the writer for these ideas on September 1, 1992.

Card #/ Idea	Hallmark	Gibson	American Greetings	Bought By	Date	Amount
1-1	8/4/92			Hallmark	9/1/92	$$$
1-2	8/4/92	8/15/92				
1-3	8/4/92	8/15/92		Gibson	9/19/92	$$$
1-4	8/4/92	8/15/92		Gibson	9/19/92	$$$
1-5	8/4/92	8/15/92				
1-6	8/4/92	8/15/92				
1-7	8/4/92	8/15/92				
1-8	8/4/92	8/15/92				
1-9	8/4/92			Hallmark	9/1/92	$$$
1-10	8/4/92	8/15/92				
2-1		8/15/92				
2-2		8/15/92		Gibson	9/19/92	$$$

Meanwhile, the writer took the eight rejects from Hallmark (numbers 1-2, 1-3, 1-4, 1-5, 1-6, 1-7 and 1-8), added two new ideas (numbers 2-1 and 2-2), and submitted this batch of ten ideas to Gibson. On September 19, 1992, Gibson purchased three of these ten, leaving seven for the writer to market elsewhere.

This chart can be refined and expanded to fit your own record-keeping needs.

WHEN YOUR IDEAS ARE PURCHASED

Most companies require writers to sign a contract stating the terms of purchase of each idea. When you sell ideas (writing) as "work for hire," you sell all copyrights, plus renewals, and extensions of that copyright. The idea becomes the exclusive property of the purchasing company. You give the company the right to use your work in any manner and for any purpose.

Sign and return the contract quickly and, usually within a week or two, you'll be paid.

Record your sales and rejections carefully. If three weeks pass after you've returned the contract, and you still haven't been paid, call to investigate. Greeting card editors have dozens of piles of paper on their desks at any given time, and your contract may be buried somewhere. However, do allow a reasonable amount of time for editors to do this paperwork. You deserve to be paid promptly for each card sold, but if you are perceived as a pest, your future sales may be jeopardized.

Study your acceptances and learn about each company's preferences. Use this information to sell even more cards the next time.

WHEN YOUR IDEAS ARE REJECTED

Ouch. Whether they're your funniest one-liners or your most soul-searching love greetings, rejections hurt. But it's essential not to take rejection personally and not to let it discourage you from trying again. You can learn as much from your rejections as you can from the cards you sell. I like to re-evaluate each idea before submitting it to another company. A few days' distance from your writing can increase your objectivity and sharpen your critical skills.

Greeting card writing has become a competitive business, and the rejection rate is high — often 80 to 90 percent. That's right — eight or nine rejects out of every ten ideas submitted.

So why do it? Because it's fun. Because you don't have to wear a suit. Because you don't have to fight traffic. Because you get a true adrenalin jolt when you *do* sell something. Because you don't have to work with people you think are jerks. Because even if you *do* get rejected, so what? They're *only* greeting cards!

Remember, each company has different standards, different markets and different needs. And if your writing is good enough, it will find a home somewhere.

If you have repeated failure with a particular company, I suggest calling and asking the editor for guidance. It may be that your writing style or formula simply does not work for that particular line. Save yourself and the editor some time by finding a new market.

Remember, too, that companies have changing policies on purchasing freelance work. In economically tough times, the freelance budget may be reduced or even eliminated. It's worthwhile to check back periodically with your clients to determine the prevailing mood toward freelance purchases.

Some larger companies balk at purchasing freelance writing because they have skilled writers on staff who can do it themselves. Editors at this type of company may actually give you the idea that they're doing you a favor by even considering looking at the writing of a lowly freelancer. This, obviously, is *not* the enlightened point of view. Cutting-edge companies realize that purchasing freelance writing breathes new life and originality into a product line. After all, freelance creators are not entrenched in the organization's politics and biases.

Contractual Arrangements

Retainer Contracts

Some companies will offer experienced writers a contract that guarantees the writers a monthly advance (or a higher fee per card purchased) in exchange for their agreement to write exclusively for that company. The writer then is obligated to provide a given amount of accepted writing each month to cover the advance. Some, including Hallmark, also offer a small monthly retainer fee that is not counted against the advance.

For example, a company may pay a contract writer a retainer fee of $100 a month. In addition to that, the writer may receive a monthly $1,000 advance. The writer is then obligated to provide at least $1,000 worth of writing to cover the company's advance. Usually, the contract writer would be paid a certain fee per piece for any work sold over and above the $1,000 advance.

There are some obvious advantages to a retainer contract. A writer can have a guaranteed monthly stipend. A company often will include contract writers on projects not open to other freelancers.

The disadvantage is that a contract limits your freedom to explore new markets. Also, if the company with whom you have the contract cuts back on its freelance budget, you're stuck with no other clients to pursue.

My personal feeling is that a retainer contract benefits the company more than the individual writer. Good social expression writers are always in demand. And if you're good enough to warrant a contract from a big company, chances are you're good enough to make it on your own.

Royalties

It is sometimes possible to negotiate a royalty arrangement with a social expression client. Companies are more open to paying royalties (usually 2 to 5 percent of gross sales) when a creator has a total concept (art and copy) to offer.

Royalty contracts should spell out your rights of ownership and the company's commitment to distribute your product. These agreements are complex, and until you're an experienced royalty negotiator, consult a lawyer before signing anything.

Once your product is on the market, the company should provide quarterly sales figures and royalty checks covering your percentage of sales for that quarter.

If you work with an artist or other partner, it is essential to have a written agreement spelling out your individual percentages of the royalties you receive.

The advantage of working for a royalty is that, if your product is successful, you will have a regular, continuing income as long as the product is in the marketplace. Also, you get to retain the copyright on your creations, and can try to sell it elsewhere when your first publisher pulls it off the shelves.

The disadvantage of working for a royalty is that you have no guarantee of income in the event of low product sales.

I think combining royalty and work for hire arrangements provides the best of both worlds for a freelancer.

MANUFACTURING YOUR OWN SOCIAL EXPRESSION PRODUCTS

If, through computer graphics, desktop publishing and artistic talent, you have the capability to produce a total social expression product (copy and design), you may want to consider manufacturing and selling the product yourself.

Whether you're interested in producing T-shirts, bumper stickers, buttons or mugs, advertising specialty companies can usually print your words and design on the products of your choice.

Be resourceful. Get several bids. Go with the vendors and suppliers who can do the best job for the best price.

There are two big disadvantages to manufacturing your own product: the initial outlay of capital, and the cumbersome task of distributing your creations to the public.

The following are some suggestions for overcoming these obstacles to self-publishing social expression products:

1. Approach a direct mail company (Lillian Vernon is a good example) about featuring your product in its catalog in exchange for a percentage of your total sales. If the company believes in you and your product, you can sometimes negotiate a purchase order guaranteeing you payment for a sizable up-front order.

2. If you have the resources, interview and hire a manufacturer's rep to sell your products. Each month, the classified ads in *Greetings* magazine list salespeople looking for social expression products to promote and sell. These people often have great connections in the industry, and their selling experience can be well worth the percentage you agree to pay them.

3. Distribute the products yourself locally. Approach the card shop at the mall and the corner drugstore about displaying your products on a consignment basis. Local messages — supporting the high school team, lambasting the politics of your community, commenting on local events — may sell off the shelves in a local retail outlet.

The "T" Word

Taxes. Because freelance income is not subject to federal withholding, it is advisable to file quarterly estimated returns. Also, if your business has shown a profit of $400 or more during a calendar year, your earnings are subject to Self-Employment Social Security Tax. That's the bad news.

The *good* news is that many income tax deductions are possible to freelancers. These include mileage to and from client meetings, research (books, magazines and other publications), postage, business equipment (and depreciation), some travel expenses, long-distance phone calls and office supplies. So save those receipts! If a portion of your home is used exclusively for your business, you are entitled to several home office deductions.

By the way, the services of a professional tax preparer are deductible, too.

Now You're All Set

Whether you're considering writing social expression as a hobby or a career, whether you're writing work for hire or producing your own products to distribute and sell, these business tips should help you get off the ground.

It's good business to be flexible and accommodating with your clients, but remember that you have a right to be treated with fairness and respect.

Although rejection is discouraging at times, writing social expression products can be emotionally and financially rewarding to those persistent, creative writers who give it their best shot. Good luck!

WORKBOOK

•M——————————————————|N|•

How to Use
the Workbook

The following pages will provide continuing help as you expand your greeting card repertoire. I encourage you to make copies of the pages you intend to use. Use a new form for each card or self-expression concept you create.

In time, these processes will come naturally to you. Until then, let these simple exercises guide you to expand your thoughts and improve your craft as a social expression writer.

The *idea starter pages* (pages 166-185) are provided to help you generate new ideas for several seasons and occasions. Use these pages as you begin writing for a particular product or sending situation. (The last idea starter page has been left blank to allow you to create your own sets of words and phrases.)

The *exercises* (pages 186-190) will be useful in helping you generate ideas and words for different kinds of cards. Use these pages to help you write in a specific style.

It is worthwhile to fill in the blanks again and again. Our minds work different ways on different days, and you'll be surprised at what different, new ideas can be triggered using the same list of words. Don't forget these helpful tools during those nonproductive moments when it's difficult to get complete, cogent thoughts down on paper. These pages may help you get unstuck in a hurry.

IDEA STARTER PAGES

Birthday

Cheer

Valentine's Day

St. Patrick's Day

Mother's Day

Father's Day

Halloween

Christmas

Self-Expression

Do-It-Yourself

EXERCISES

Traditional Greeting Card
  — Organizer/Worksheet

Traditional Humorous/Illustrated
  — Rebus Worksheet

Cute and New Humor Cards
  — Thinking Visually

SAMPLE NEEDS LIST (ACME GREETINGS)

GREETING CARD WRITER'S LIBRARY

BIRTHDAY IDEA STARTER PAGE

Possible Sending Situations:

To Friend

To Relative

Age-Specific—30, 40, 50

Over the Hill

To Spouse/Significant Other

Belated

To Co-Worker

To Child

To _____

To _____

To _____

To _____

Key Words:

Cake	Day Off	Joy
Ice Cream	Party	Contentment
Celebrate	Party Animal	Great Year
Candles	Party Hats	Young at Heart
Presents	Balloons	_____
Six-Pack	Confetti	_____
Treats	Champagne	_____
Wrinkles	Chocolate	_____
Gray Hair	Wishes	_____
Weight	Birthday Song	_____
Games	Over the Hill	_____
Happiness	Crazy	_____
Fun	Excuse My Forgetting	_____

Opening Lines:

☛ It's your birthday!
Party till _____

☛ Don't think of it as getting older . . .

☛ Are those your birthday candles?

☛ You're HOW old?

☛ Happy Birthday to the one
who_____!

☛ _____

☛ _____

☛ _____

☛ _____

☛ _____

☛ _____

☛ _____

☛ _____

CHEER IDEA STARTER PAGE

Possible Sending Situations:

Get Well

Thinking of You

Hospital

Operation

Accident

Humorous Get Well

Seriously Ill

Nursing Home Resident

_____

_____

Key Words:

Get Well	Quack	Flowers
Sunshine	Stitches	Bouquet
Fresh Air	Nurses	Affection
Relax	Bedpans	Care
Lots of Rest	Gowns	Concern
T.L.C.	Shots	_____
Vitamins	Blood Pressure	_____
Medicine	Comfortable	_____
Fever	Peaceful	_____
Flu	Hospital Bed	_____
Chills	Warm Thoughts	_____
Bills	Feeling Better	_____
Doctor	Feeling Lousy	_____

Opening Lines:

☛ Sorry you're under the weather . . .

☛ Being in the hospital isn't so bad . . .

☛ You know what's worse than being sick?

☛ Don't let your doctor fool you!

☛ Is there anything I can do to help you feel better?

☛ _____

☛ _____

☛ _____

☛ _____

☛ _____

☛ _____

☛ _____

☛ _____

VALENTINE'S DAY IDEA STARTER PAGE

Possible Sending Situations:

Romantic

Humorous

Mom

Other Relative

Friendship

Juvenile Packaged

Juvenile Individual

_____

_____

_____

_____

Key Words:

Hugs	Date	Personals
Kisses	Be Mine	Marriage
Love	Horny	Mr. Right
Lust	Enchantment	Heaven
Candy	Infatuation	Love Goddess
Hearts	Holding Hands	_____
Candy Hearts	New Love	_____
Romance	Old Love	_____
Cupid	Tunnel of Love	_____
Flowers	Love Songs	_____
Affair	Hunks	_____
Sex	Heavy Petting	_____
Embrace	Sweetheart	_____

Opening Lines:

☛ Either you be my Valentine, or . . .

☛ Of *course* I love you!

☛ What could be better than being Valentines with you?

☛ Wishing you the perfect Valentine fantasy . . .

☛ Love me! Thrill me! Kiss me!

☛ _____

☛ _____

☛ _____

☛ _____

☛ _____

☛ _____

☛ _____

☛ _____

St. Patrick's Day Idea Starter Page

Possible Sending Situations:

Friend

Relative

Irish to Irish

Non-Irish to Irish

Humorous

_____

_____

_____

_____

_____

Key Words:

Green	Heritage	_____
Green Beer	History	_____
Shamrocks	Rainbow	_____
Shillelaghs	Pot O'Gold	_____
Dublin	Irish Eyes	_____
Ireland	Top O'the Mornin'	_____
Driving Snakes Out of Ireland		_____
O'Leary	Lucky	_____
Parade	Parties	_____
Celebrate	Rosie O'Grady	_____
Emerald Isle	Great Day For the Irish	_____
Leprechaun	Four-Leaf Clover	_____
Irish Names	Twinkling Eyes	_____

Opening Lines:

☛ It's a great day for the wearin' of the green . . .

☛ As old Casey O'Grady used to say . . .

☛ A traditional Irish wish for you on St. Patrick's Day . . .

☛ At the end of every rainbow, may you find . . .

☛ _____

☛ _____

☛ _____

☛ _____

☛ _____

☛ _____

☛ _____

☛ _____

MOTHER'S DAY IDEA STARTER PAGE

Possible Sending Situations:

To Mom

To Grandma

To Wife

Kid to Mom

Kid to Grandma

To Friend

Humorous

_____

_____

_____

_____

_____

Key Words:

Hugs	Budget	Sex
Pampering	Shopping	Friends
Take It Easy	Marriage	Naps
Day Off	Pregnancy	Babysitters
PTA Meeting	Empty Nest	Good Advice
Good Listener	Nurturing	_____
Kids Fighting	T.L.C.	_____
Housework	Sacrifices	_____
Stretch Marks	Carpools	_____
Laundry	Boo-Boo Fixer	_____
Working Mom	Single Moms	_____
Juggling Time	Curfew	_____
Home Cooking	Minivans	_____

Opening Lines:

☞ You're that certain special kind of mom . . .

☞ It's your special day, Mom, so go ahead —

☞ Wishing you a day that's every mother's dream . . .

☞ Happy Mother's Day to a mom
who has a way with _____ .

☞ Happy Mother's Day from your little _____ .

☞ _____

☞ _____

☞ _____

☞ _____

☞ _____

☞ _____

☞ _____

☞ _____

FATHER'S DAY IDEA STARTER PAGE

Possible Sending Situations:

To Dad

To Grandpa

To Husband

Humorous

Kid to Dad

Kid to Grandpa

_____

_____

_____

_____

_____

Key Words:

Handyman	Daughter's Dates	Advice
Allowance	Thermostat	Football
Loans	Discipline	Playing Catch
Golf	Back Talk	Shooting Hoops
Clothing	Credit Cards	Briefcase
Fishing	Single Dad	_____
Guidance	Snoring	_____
Role Model	Dad's Cooking	_____
Homework	Barbecues	_____
Business Trips	Dad as Daycare	_____
Nap on Couch	Dear Old Dad	_____
Remote Control	Father	_____
Curfew	Do as I Say . . .	_____

Opening Lines:

☛ Dad, you're one in a million . . .

☛ I'll never forget those valuable words of advice, Dad . . .

☛ Happy Father's Day to the father of my children . . .

☛ You deserve a break today, Dad . . .

☛ Remember the cardinal rule of parenting . . .

☛ _____

☛ _____

☛ _____

☛ _____

☛ _____

☛ _____

☛ _____

☛ _____

HALLOWEEN IDEA STARTER PAGE

Possible Sending Situations:

To Friend

To Love Interest

Juvenile

Humorous

_____

_____

_____

_____

_____

Key Words:

Black Cat	Dracula	Zombies
Witch	Vampire	Tomb
Broom	Coffin	Skeleton
Spell	Blood	Scary
Brew	Fangs	Bones
Ghost	Cobwebs	Chain Saw
Boo	Pumpkin	_____
Haunted House	Jack O'Lantern	_____
Trick or Treat	Party	_____
Candy	Bob for Apples	_____
Costumes	Midnight	_____
Masks	Frankenstein	_____
Cemetery	Monsters	_____

Opening Lines:

☛ Want to come over at midnight and bob for . . .

☛ You know what's *really* scary on Halloween?

☛ Guess what this witch is doing?

☛ Jason wants *you* to have a Happy Halloween!

☛ _____

☛ _____

☛ _____

☛ _____

☛ _____

☛ _____

☛ _____

☛ _____

CHRISTMAS IDEA STARTER PAGE

Possible Sending Situations:

Family

Across the Miles

Friend

Spouse/Significant Other

Boxed Cards

_____

_____

_____

_____

_____

Key Words:

Holly	Reindeer	Decorations
Deck the Halls	Fruitcake	Tinsel
Fa-La-La-La-La	Family Times	Lights
Shopping	Carols	Mistletoe
Malls	Eggnog	Church
Crowds	Baby Jesus	_____
Snow	Manger	_____
Snowman	Shepherds	_____
Snow Angels	Star	_____
Chimney	Wise Men	_____
Santa Claus	Bethlehem	_____
Stockings	Tiny Tim	_____
Gifts	Children	_____

Opening Lines:

☞ All I want for Christmas is . . .

☞ I've got some good news and some bad news
for you this Christmas . . .

☞ I love the holidays . . .

☞ I'll bet I know what *you* want in your stocking this year . . .

☞ _____

☞ _____

☞ _____

☞ _____

☞ _____

☞ _____

☞ _____

☞ _____

SELF-EXPRESSION IDEA STARTER PAGE

Use this sheet to create a target consumer for your self-expression products.

PRODUCT CATEGORY (T-shirt, bumper sticker, button, etc.):

MARKET:

Age: _____ Teen _____ 20-35 _____ 35-50 _____ 50-65 _____ 65+

Sex: _____ M _____ F

Other demographic information:

WHAT DO I WANT TO SAY TO THE WORLD?

WHAT ARE MY POLITICS?

(Choose one or more)

Conservative	Liberal
Pro-Life	Pro-Choice
Anti-Porn	Anti-Censorship
Pro-Religion	Pro-Humanism
Pro-U.S.A.	Environmentalist
Pro-Nukes	World Peace
Right to Bear Arms	Gun Control

WHAT DO I LIKE?

(Choose one or more)

Chocolate	Soap Operas	Aerobics	Beer
Ice Cream	Game Shows	Tennis	Wine
Pizza	Talk Shows	Golf	Dieting
Running	Rock and Roll	Fishing	_____
Walking	Jazz	Bowling	_____

WHAT AM I MAD AT?

Loud music

Nuclear reactors

Drunk drivers

Censorship

Taxes

My Kids

My Parents

_____

_____

WHAT CAN I BRAG ABOUT?

Children

Grandchildren

Boyfriend

Pets

Local sports team

Car

_____

_____

AM I PROUD OF MY VOCATION?

Doctor	Lawyer
Cowboy	MBA
Nurse	Construction Worker
Teacher	Programmer
Secretary	Salesperson
Accountant	Dentist

DO-IT-YOURSELF IDEA STARTER PAGE

Possible Sending Situations:

_____

_____

_____

_____

_____

_____

_____

_____

_____

_____

Key Words:

Opening Lines:

☛ _____

☛ _____

☛ _____

☛ _____

☛ _____

☛ _____

☛ _____

☛ _____

☛ _____

☛ _____

☛ _____

TRADITIONAL GREETING CARD

ORGANIZER/WORKSHEET

Use this form to get organized and focused before writing a card. The information and thoughts on this paper will make the blank page less intimidating.

WHO IS SENDING THIS CARD?

Age _____ Sex _____ Occupation _____

Demographics _____

Other info _____

_____

WHO IS RECEIVING IT?

Age _____ Sex _____ Occupation _____

Demographics _____

Other info _____

_____

Relationship to sender _____

_____

What is the sending situation (life event, occasion, season, or non-occasion reason for sending)? _____

_____

What is the sender's message to the recipient (feelings, wishes, comments, key words)? _____

_____

_____

What seasonal or natural imagery will you include in your writing?

_____

_____

_____

_____

What structure or formula will you use to communicate this message poetically and logically? _____

_____

_____

IF WRITING VERSE:

From sender's message (above), what are likely rhyme words for this card? _____

_____

What rhyme scheme will you work with? _____

In what meter should the card be written? _____

Notes: _____

_____

_____

_____

_____

_____

TRADITIONAL HUMOROUS/ILLUSTRATED

REBUS WORKSHEET

Use this worksheet to organize your thoughts when writing a rebus.

What metaphor, simile or concept will you use?
(Uncles are like horses, your baby is the boss, etc.)

_____

_____

Fill out the following form to flesh out the concept. (E.g., in what specific ways are uncles like horses and is your baby the boss?) Refer to Chapter Nine to see a completed chart.

HUMOROUS/ILLUSTRATED CONCEPT:	
IMAGES:	WORDS:

What are some good opening lines? _____

_____

_____

_____

_____

What are some punchy, preferably complimentary, closing lines? ___

_____

_____

What are some good rhyme words for this concept? _____

_____

_____

_____

_____

What rhyme scheme will you use? _____

_____

What meter and/or structure? _____

_____

Notes: _____

_____

_____

_____

_____

_____

_____

CUTE AND NEW HUMOR CARDS

THINKING VISUALLY

This exercise will be helpful when you write cute or new humor cards. Being as creative and innovative as you can be, describe or draw original visual interpretations of each of the following standard greeting card messages. When you've thought of visual ideas for each message, go back and write new, creative, innovative copy to go with the visuals.

This moving back and forth between visual and editorial is an essential skill for greeting card writers.

Thinking of you	Happy birthday
I'm glad we're friends	I'm sorry
Happy anniversary	Thank you
I love you	Happy holidays
Congratulations	Just to say "hello"

SAMPLE NEEDS LIST

ACME GREETINGS HUMOR

Following is a typical letter that you might receive (or solicit) from a greeting card company describing their current needs:

Dear Freelancer:

We are looking for fresh, new humor ideas (verse and prose) for the following everyday captions:

BIRTHDAY:	CHEER:	ANNIVERSARY:
To Relative	Get Well	Workplace
General Wish	Cope	
Celebrate		
Age Slam		

We are also beginning to plan next year's Valentine's Day and St. Patrick's Day card lines. Please send material for the following captions:

VALENTINE'S DAY:	ST. PATRICK'S DAY
Love	General Wish
Friendship	Love
To Wife/Husband	
Suggestive	

Please type your card ideas on three-by-five-inch index cards and submit in batches of ten to:
Freelance Editor
Acme Greetings
City, State

Enclose a self-addressed, stamped envelope.

GREETING CARD WRITER'S LIBRARY

THE WRITER'S MARKET. F&W Publications, Inc., 1507 Dana Ave., Cincinnati, OH 45207. Available in a new edition each year, this is an up-to-date source of information on publishers' (including greeting card companies') needs and guidelines.

HUMOR AND CARTOON MARKET. F&W Publications, Inc., 1507 Dana Ave., Cincinnati, OH 45207. Published annually, this is an up-to-date source of information about publishers of humorous material, including cartoons.

GREETINGS magazine. 309 5th Ave., New York, NY 10016. The industry publication. Includes information on new product lines, personnel changes, and retail marketing of greeting card companies.

GREETING CARD INDUSTRY DIRECTORY. The Greeting Card Association, 1350 New York Avenue NW, Suite 615, Washington, D.C. 20005. Phone: (202) 393-1778. Available bi-annually from the Greeting Card Association, this book lists names, addresses and product lines of all exhibitors at the National (New York) Stationery Show.

THE COMPLETE RHYMING DICTIONARY. Edited by Clement Wood. Doubleday & Co., Inc., Garden City, NY. If you intend to write humorous or serious verse, this book is a must.

BARTLETT'S FAMILIAR QUOTATIONS. Little, Brown and Co., 34 Beacon Street, Boston, MA 02106. An excellent source of idea-starter material as well as public domain quotations to include when submitting inspirational writing.

ROGET'S INTERNATIONAL THESAURUS. Thomas Y. Crowell Company, 10 E. 53rd Street, New York, NY 10022. Each entry and subsequent word list is a potential idea starter. Also helps you avoid those "tired" greeting card words.

YOUR FAVORITE DICTIONARY. Learn to love your dictionary. It's a source of ideas as well as grammatical and spelling assistance.

INDEX

A

A-A-B-B rhyme scheme, 54
A-B-C-B rhyme scheme, 54
Activity cards, juvenile, 77
Adjectives, 17
Adult baptism, 67
Affirmations, 70
Allegory, 20-21
Alliteration, 22, 62, 75-76
Alternative
  greeting cards, 7, 100, 110
  humor, 46
  inspirational, 70-71
Anapest, 52
Anniversary cards
  general, 33
  our wedding, 33
  wedding, 32-33
Answering machines, 149
Anyday cards (*see* everyday cards)
Audience, 86, 127

B

Baby congratulation cards, 36
Barry Manilow's Greatest Hits, 53
Bartlett's Familiar Quotations, 43
Beats, 50
Birthday cards, 29-30
  close relationship, 30-31, 46
  compliment, 30
  general, 30
  idea starters, 166-167
  miscellaneous, 31
  relative, 31-32, 41, 86-88
  religious, 67
  special, 31

Books, 142-143
Bradley, Amanda, 68
Bumper stickers, 135-136
Buttons, 136-137

C

Calendars, 133-134
Captions, 28, 92-93, 132
  risque, 136
Car window signs, 137
Checkbook covers, 137
Cheer cards
  get well, 34
  hospital, 34-35
  idea starters, 168-169
  thinking of you, 35
Chocolate, 19-20, 22, 40
Christmas cards
  boxed, 45-46
  idea starters, 180-181
  individual, 46, 67-68
Chronic Fatigue Syndrome brainstorm, 111-112
Clothing, 134-135
Combs, 137
Communication, difficulty of, 102
Competition, 158
Complete Rhyming Dictionary, The, 50
Computer, 136, 148
Concept work, 80, 115-116
Congratulation cards, 36, 42
Contractual arrangements, 158-160
Copyright law, 43, 143-144, 154-156
Couplet, 54
Creative process, 10
Creativity, 14, 18

T

U

V

W

Other Books of Interest

Annual Market Books

Artist's Market, edited by Lauri Miller $22.95

Children's Writer's & Illustrator's Market, edited by Lisa Carpenter (paper) $17.95

Guide to Literary Agents & Art/Photo Reps, edited by Robin Gee $15.95

Humor & Cartoon Markets, edited by Bob Staake (paper) $18.95

Novel & Short Story Writer's Market, edited by Robin Gee (paper) $19.95

Poet's Market, by Judson Jerome $19.95

Songwriter's Market, edited by Brian Rushing $19.95

Writer's Market, edited by Mark Kissling $26.95

General Writing Books

Beginning Writer's Answer Book, edited by Kirk Polking (paper) $13.95

Discovering the Writer Within, by Bruce Ballenger & Barry Lane $17.95

Freeing Your Creativity, by Marshall Cook $17.95

Make Your Words Work, by Gary Provost $17.95

The 28 Biggest Writing Blunders, by William Noble $12.95

The 29 Most Common Writing Mistakes & How To Avoid Them, by Judy Delton (paper) $9.95

The Writer's Book of Checklists, by Scott Edelstein $16.95

The Writer's Digest Guide to Manuscript Formats, by Buchman & Groves $18.95

The Writer's Essential Desk Reference, edited by Glenda Neff $19.95

Nonfiction Writing

Creative Conversations: The Writer's Guide to Conducting Interviews, by Michael Schumacher $16.95

How to Do Leaflets, Newsletters & Newspapers, by Nancy Brigham (paper) $14.95

How to Sell Every Magazine Article You Write, by Lisa Collier Cool (paper) $11.95

The Magazine Article: How To Think It, Plan It, Write It, by Peter Jacobi $17.95

The Writer's Digest Handbook of Magazine Article Writing, edited by Jean M. Fredette (paper) $11.95

Fiction Writing

Characters & Viewpoint, by Orson Scott Card $13.95

The Complete Guide to Writing Fiction, by Barnaby Conrad $18.95

Creating Characters: How To Build Story People, by Dwight V. Swain $16.95

Dialogue, by Lewis Turco $13.95

The Fiction Writer's Silent Partner, by Martin Roth $19.95

Manuscript Submission, by Scott Edelstein $13.95

Mastering Fiction Writing, by Kit Reed $18.95

Plot, by Ansen Dibell $13.95

Theme & Strategy, by Ronald B. Tobias $13.95

The 38 Most Common Fiction Writing Mistakes, by Jack M. Bickham $12.95

Writer's Digest Handbook of Novel Writing, $18.95

Special Interest Writing Books

Comedy Writing Secrets, by Mel Helitzer (paper) $15.95

The Complete Book of Feature Writing, by Leonard Witt $18.95

Complete Guide to Greeting Card Design & Illustration, by Eva Szela $29.95

Creating Poetry, by John Drury $18.95

How to Write & Sell True Crime, by Gary Provost $17.95

How to Write Mysteries, by Shannon OCork $13.95

How to Write Romances, by Phyllis Taylor Pianka $15.95

How to Write Science Fiction & Fantasy, Orson Scott Card $13.95

Powerful Business Writing, by Tom McKeown $12.95

Successful Scriptwriting, by Jurgen Wolff & Kerry Cox (paper) $14.95

Writing the Modern Mystery, by Barbara Norville (paper) $12.95

The Writing Business

The Complete Guide to Self-Publishing, by Tom & Marilyn Ross (paper) $16.95

Business & Legal Forms for Authors & Self-Publishers, by Tad Crawford (paper) $4.99

The Writer's Guide to Self-Promotion & Publicity, by Elane Feldman $16.95

Writing A to Z, edited by Kirk Polking $24.95

To order directly from the publisher, include $3.00 postage and handling for 1 book and $1.00 for each additional book. Allow 30 days for delivery.

Writer's Digest Books, 1507 Dana Avenue, Cincinnati, Ohio 45207
Credit card orders call TOLL-FREE
1-800-289-0963
Prices subject to change without notice.

Write to this same address for information on *Writer's Digest* magazine, *Story* magazine, Writer's Digest Book Club, Writer's Digest School, and Writer's Digest Criticism Service.